Thematic Patterns
in Sonatas of
BEETHOVEN

Thematic Patterns
in Sonatas of
BEETHOVEN

RUDOLPH RÉTI

Edited by Deryck Cooke

Da Capo Press • New York • 1992

Library of Congress Cataloging in Publication Data

Reti, Rudolph, 1885-1957.
  Thematic patterns in sonatas of Beethoven / Rudolph Reti;
edited by Deryck Cooke.
      p.   cm.—(Music reprint series)
  Reprint. Originally published: New York: Macmillan, 1967.
  ISBN 0-306-79714-3
  1. Beethoven, Ludwig van, 1770-1827. Sonatas, piano. 2.
Sonatas (Piano)—Analysis, appreciation. I. Cooke, Deryck. II. Ti-
tle. III. Series: Da Capo Press music reprint series.
MT145.B42R35   1992
786.2′183—dc20
                                                    90-39960
                                                       CIP

This Da Capo Press reprint edition of *Thematic Patterns in
Sonatas of Beethoven* is an unabridged republication of the edition
published in New York in 1967. It is reprinted by arrangement
with Macmillan Publishing Co.

Published by Da Capo Press, Inc.
A Subsidiary of Plenum Publishing Corporation
233 Spring Street, New York, N.Y. 10013

Manufactured in the United States of America

Preface

For more than thirty years Rudolph Réti had been fascinated by problems of musical structure, but not until 1944 did he begin a systematic study of the thematic process—a study which was to continue throughout the thirteen remaining years of his life.

From 1944 to 1948, he devoted himself to works of Beethoven, and it was during those years that the analyses contained in the present volume were made. In these analyses, Réti set forth some principles of composition: motivic permeation, the transformation of themes, the thematic relationship of all themes in all movements; above all, he demonstrated that in each work Beethoven established *a thematic pattern*, which served as an over-all architectural plan governing not only the themes themselves, but the bridges, figurations, harmonies, modulations, and even to some extent, the rhythm.

As an outgrowth of these studies, Réti wrote *The Thematic Process in Music* (Macmillan, New York, 1951, and Faber and Faber, London, 1961). In this book he traced the development of the thematic principle from its beginnings to the present time, using some of the Beethoven analyses made earlier.

At his death in 1957, Réti left in manuscript his just completed *Tonality—Atonality—Pantonality*. As his widow and musical executor, my first task was to see that book through the press (Rockliff, London, 1958, and Macmillan, New York, 1958).

Later, heartened by the widespread interest in Réti's writings, I wished to present the remaining analyses in book form under the title: *Thematic Patterns in Sonatas of Beethoven*. In the light of terminology subsequently developed in *The Thematic Process*, I made some changes to ensure consistency; I also deleted some examples when a point had already been made clear in *The Thematic Process*. But apart from very minor changes, the text is Rudolph Réti's and represents his thought during the years 1944 to 1948.

From an intimate sharing of his life and work, I know that Réti was

7

ever ready to revise his position; he was mindful of music as a living, flowing body of sound. Thus he encouraged students not to accept his words as graven in stone, but rather to consider them as creative insights, flexible insights, by which the listener, the performer and the composer might be stimulated to new discoveries for themselves. 'A work of musical art,' said Réti, 'is determined by laws so strict, logical and organic that it becomes in itself an allegory of all creation.'

I should like to thank the many friends and admirers of Rudolph Réti who encouraged me in my work on the present book—Egon Wellesz especially gave constant support and advice. A grant from the Jay Hambridge Foundation and a grant from the Canada Council helped to make my work possible. My continued gratitude goes to Donald Mitchell, of Faber and Faber, London, and to Cecil Scott, of The Macmillan Company, New York. To Deryck Cooke go my warmest thanks for his Introduction and notes, and for the perception and enthusiasm with which he undertook his editorial tasks.

August 27, 1966, JEAN RÉTI-FORBES
University of Georgia,
Athens, Georgia.

Contents

CONTENTS

CONTENTS

Tempo of the *Grave* Sounding from the *Allegro*
A Thematic Song

SECTION 2—THEMATIC STRUCTURE AND FORM

SECTION 3—THEMATIC ARCHITECTURE

CHAPTER 13. ARCHITECTURAL PLANNING

CONTENTS

Editor's Introduction

MY admiration for Rudolph Réti's profound insight into the processes of musical creation, which was awakened by a reading of *The Thematic Process in Music*, has been deepened further by editing this present book for publication. It offers exhaustive analyses of two works only touched on in *The Thematic Process*—the *Pathétique* and *Appassionata* sonatas—as well as more general analyses of three other Beethoven sonatas, and two final chapters of illuminating but dispersed reflections which he would no doubt have put into more coherent shape if he had lived.

The far-reaching concepts which arise from the analyses are even more important than the analyses themselves; but one or two warnings may be helpful to the reader trained in the traditional method of analysis associated with Sir Donald Tovey. Although Réti employs the traditional terms 'exposition', 'development' and 'recapitulation' for the large-scale divisions of sonata form, he does not use the traditional terms for the smaller-scale divisions, such as 'first subject', 'transition', 'second subject', and so on—for reasons he himself gives in Chapter 12. Or rather, he does use certain of them—'subject', 'group', and 'section', for example—but in a rather different sense; and this should be kept in mind if misunderstanding is to be avoided.

In the matter of key, the reader may be occasionally puzzled by what appear to be simple inaccuracies, unless he realizes that Réti is often concerned with what he calls the 'thematic pitch' of a theme or section or movement, as opposed to its tonality. Thus the 'thematic pitch' of the first theme of the Sonata *Appassionata* is C, although its tonality is F minor; in other words, the theme revolves around the dominant. I have added a footnote wherever there seems the possibility of a misunderstanding on this point.

Resistance to the type of analytic method used by Réti is common, and the reader would be well advised to try to keep an open mind until the argument is fully established. For example, objections to certain initial concepts in the analysis of the *Pathétique* can be retrospectively made to appear irrelevant by the time one encounters Example 56, with its masterly demonstration of the unity of all the contrasting themes of the first movement, and more so by Examples 127 and 134.

As regards the familiar question 'What possible help can this kind of analysis give the ordinary music-lover in the matter of understanding and enjoying the music ?', I can only answer by quoting one case amongst several which have come to my notice. When I once acted as a member of the panel in the BBC feature 'Music Questions', we were faced with a question from one puzzled listener as to the relationship of the passage shown in Réti's Example 69 to the rest of the first movement of the *Pathétique*: he was worried by it because it seemed to him to have no connection with the argument. Whether he was satisfied with the answer we gave him I don't know; but if he buys this book he will certainly find full illumination in what Réti has to say about Example 69 —illumination which cannot be found in any analysis of this work according to the traditional method.

DERYCK COOKE

27th September, 1965

Section 1
The Thematic Pattern of the *Pathétique*

I

The Opening of the *Grave*
Introduction

1. GENERAL CONCEPT OF MUSICAL CELLS

EVERY musical composition on a high structural level contains
several motivic cells from which its structure is formed. These cells
need not necessarily be identical with the concrete motifs. In some
compositions the cells may not even be visible in their literal form. The
motifs, and subsequently the themes, are developed from the cells; the
cells, however, usually represent the essence of the motifs rather than the
motifs themselves.*

2. THE PRIME CELLS OF THE *PATHÉTIQUE*

The prime cells of the *Pathétique* are:

Example 1

However, in order to distinguish easily between the two, the term
prime cell will in this analysis be applied to the first cell only. The second
cell will be called the *concluding motif*, since the composer uses it almost
invariably whenever he concludes a section, a period, or sometimes even
a phrase.

The basic thematic idea of the *Pathétique*, the core of its structural life,
will be found to be a combination of *these two cells*. It will be seen that all
the shapes throughout the whole sonata—the themes, groups and
sections—are formed from, and are variants of, these two elements. We
may therefore present the basic structural scheme of the *Pathétique* as:
prime cell plus concluding motif.

* In this connection the cell is not to be regarded as a (so to say) mystical
phenomenon from which the composer builds his work, but rather as a variant
of a motif, the variant which represents the shortest extract of a motif, its contour.

3. INVERSIONS AND TRANSPOSITIONS

The cells appear, in almost every composition, not only in their original form, but also as *inversions*.★ Therefore, we see the following forms in the *Pathétique*:

Example 2

Naturally, in any lengthy composition the cells frequently appear *transposed* to different pitches.

4. CELLS AT WORK

An examination of the melodic line formed by the four opening bars of the *Pathétique* (see Example 4) shows, even at a first glance, that it contains a series of rising prime cells, followed by a descending passage.

In detail, bar 1 expresses the prime cell in its basic key. Bar 2 then repeats bar 1 at a higher pitch. At what pitch? At precisely the one which makes the interval between the two bars, that is D to F, again an expression of the prime cell (transposed).†

The two following bars repeat the first two. In order, however, to increase tempo and dynamics, the first motif sounds twice within bar 3 alone. Then again a prime cell interval follows, just as between bar 1 and 2, but this time filled in:

Example 3

(a)

and crowned by the following

(b)

corresponding to bar 2.

★ Strictly speaking, the term contrary motion rather than inversion should be applied to some of the figures above. For the sake of simplicity, however, one term may here be used for both.

[† Réti means the interval between the D which *ends* the first bar and the F which *begins* the second.—ED.]

Here the peak of the climax is reached, and the aforementioned descending passage concludes the group. And even in this passage the prime cell again appears embroidered, immediately, at the top:

Now let us extract the melodic content of this descending passage. Apart from the many interwoven prime cells, we recognize the overall contour to be our second cell, *the concluding motif*:

and indeed, it concludes the opening period of the *Pathétique*.

To sum up, the following schematic outline emerges:

Example 4

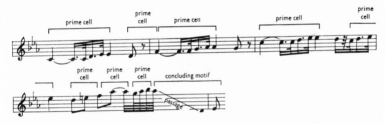

Thus, even in this first brief survey, the melodic line of the opening bars is seen to consist of the *prime cell*—in fact, an uninterrupted series of prime cells, *plus the concluding motif*.

5. VOICE BY VOICE, BAR BY BAR

Having gone through this first and rather sweeping survey, we may now proceed to more concrete detail. Our next task, therefore, will be to uncover, voice by voice and bar by bar, the material from which the opening period is built.

Starting with the soprano part, let us look at the first bar once again. This bar forms, as was said, an expression of the prime cell. Actually, however, only its first part represents the cell itself, and we will henceforth call this part the *prime motif*. The second part of the bar is formed by another particle, which, in the course of the work, will also turn out to be a motif.* We may call it the *finishing motif*,† since it finishes the phrase.

Example 5

Apart from these two motifs (the prime motif and the finishing motif), no other shape whatsoever appears in the soprano part until the passage expressing the concluding motif is heard. And going to the limit of analytical dissection, we could even resolve the detail of this passage as a series of finishing motifs followed by two prime cells and their inversions:

Example 6

Proceeding to the bass (Example 7), in the first bar we discover the prime cell again, followed first by its inversion, then by an inversion of the finishing motif. Yet this does not cover the whole content of the bar. There still remains the leap from C to F sharp. However, by connecting

Example 7

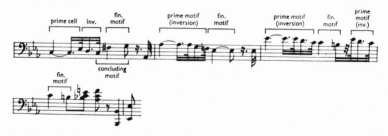

* We call any musical element a motif—be it a melodic fragment or sometimes only a rhythmical or dynamic feature—which, through constantly being repeated and varied throughout a work, or a section of it, assumes a similar role in the compositional design to that of a motif in the fine arts or in literature.

† The reader is asked to refrain from analysing this 'term' and various other terms of a similar kind. They are chosen almost at random, for the sake of conciseness only.

the following G to this, we easily recognize the inversion of the concluding motif. Thus here again we have our basic phenomenon—prime cell plus concluding motif—this time even concentrated into the short space of the very first bar.

Then, as the bass continues, in bar 2 the simple pattern of prime motif (inversion) plus finishing motif appears. Before this, however, a new feature is heard—namely an *auftakt* (up-beat) in the form of a leap from A flat to its octave. We therefore list this octave as a new motif:

Example 8

Bar 3 repeats the foregoing; bar 4 then divides the bass into three lines, and at the risk of becoming almost pedantic, let us examine each of them. The upper line:

Example 9

consists of the finishing motif plus the concluding motif. The middle line:

consists of the finishing motif plus its inversion—after which a note-repetition at the unison follows. We now list both the unison and the octave as one motif and its inversion, and call this motif the *note-repetition*. The lower line:

consists of a prime cell in inversion, but changed from the original *minor to major*—a feature which at this point in the analysis should be accepted simply as a fact (the significance of it will soon be realized). New, too, is the form in which the cell is here expressed, a chromatic note having been added to the familiar shape. We will call it the *prime motif in chromatic form.* The remainder of this bar proceeds again in one line. It reads:

that is, the concluding motif in a slightly varied form.

The prime cell is also at work in the beginning of the tenor line:

Example 10

The motif of note-repetition, now already familiar to us, plus the finishing motif (inversion) forms the remainder of the first bar. During the next bar the figure of note-repetition comes to the fore, thus clearly proving the thematic character of this little element. In bar 3 and in the beginning of bar 4 the inversion of the prime cell in the major, also familiar to us, appears.

The shape of the last voice to be examined, the alto, is very close to that of the tenor.

Example 11

These two voices, being the least exposed, favour the inconspicuous motif of note-repetition. Still, both the prime cell and the concluding motif, the sonata's basic elements, are of course also to be seen.

6. LIST OF MOTIFS

The preceding survey, then, provides the following list of motifs:

Example 12

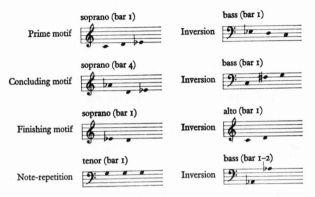

To this we have to add, as variants, the prime cell in the major, the prime motif in chromatic form, and the concluding motif in varied form.

This is the whole list,★ and it certainly reduces to transparent clarity material which at first may have seemed exceedingly complicated. Its real significance, however, and the reason why we did not hesitate to go through this somewhat tiresome enumeration, lies deeper—namely in its completeness. For this small list of four motifs covers *every note in every voice of this opening period.* Just as in a fugue of Bach, though there effected through a different technique, nothing remains outside the structural unity.

★ It may be interesting to realize that even these few shapes may be resolved into two, since the concluding motif may be understood as a summation of two prime cells in inversion plus the finishing motif:

Example 13

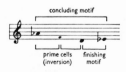

2

The Continuation of the *Grave* Introduction

1. CONTINUING MOTIVIC UNITY

THE continuing motivic unity and strictness in the following section can now be charted. Again the essence of the matter lies in the fact that every note is included in the motivic scheme:

Example 14

2. THEMATIC CONTOUR

The opening period concludes, according to tradition, in the relative major (E flat, bar 5). Thus the relationship between these two groups as a whole expresses the prime cell (C to E flat). And that Beethoven really meant it this way is further proved by the bass line of bar 5, which after the long sustained E flat falls to the D, forming the finishing motif (E flat to D).

Thus the first five bars of the sonata reflect the first bar in a wide arc— or in other words, prime cell plus finishing motif here sounds as a thematic contour from the first five bars of the work:*

Example 15

3. THE PRIME CELL IN THE MAJOR

In bar 5 the key changes to the major. Therefore, if the composer wished, in the continuance of his melodic line, to cling to his original motif at all, it was necessary to change the motif itself to the major shape. This is exactly what happens in the sonata:

Example 16

and since this certainly appears as a natural, self-evident musical procedure, the idea of a prime cell in two shapes, one in the minor and one in the major, also becomes a plausible and organic phenomenon.

The prime cell in the major appears both in its original form and in its inversions:

Example 17

* Cf. 'The Conception of a Thematic Contour', p. 93, *The Thematic Process in Music*, Rudolph Réti.

4. NEW FACES—OLD MOTIFS

In bar 6 the following shape emerges:

Example 18

prime motif   finishing
motif

What is this? In so far as the melodic line is concerned, we recognize it as the old shape of bar 1: prime motif plus finishing motif. Yet our ear would be inclined to register it as something new. The explanation is that, though the melodic line has been retained, rhythm and accent have been shifted. In bar 1 the strongest accent fell on the first note, but in the new form it appears as an *auftakt* without any particular accent.

Still further prime motivic shapes, this time in chromatic form, are seen in bars 7 and 8. Here, too, through shifts of rhythm and accent, similar and even stronger changes of face are brought about, as follows:

Example 19

prime motif   prime motif

Such a method of changing the character of an old motif by transforming its rhythmical idea, fulfils two contrasting but equally important goals: first, to preserve the structural continuity by employing the old motif; second, to achieve variety by changing its outward appearance.

Another example of a somewhat similar, though not quite identical technique is seen in bar 5. Here the octave leap, which originally stood outside the bar as an *auftakt*, now appears within the bar as a part of the motif itself:

Example 20

But perhaps this example already belongs to our next topic of discussion.

5. INTERWOVEN MOTIFS

We have already seen the technique of interweaving motifs at work in bar 4, where, from the top of the passage expressing the concluding motif, the prime motif also sounds through:

Example 21

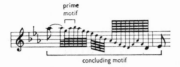

Here the concluding motif (A flat, D, E flat) forms the contour of the passage, into which the transposed prime motif (G, A flat, B flat) is interwoven.

A similar phenomenon becomes visible in bar 9:

Example 22

The essence of this phrase, too, is the concluding motif (F, B, C), and here another motif, namely that of note-repetition, is interwoven. Moreover, a second shape of the concluding motif, or rather a variant of it, comes into existence within the first, through a suddenly introduced alto voice—B, F, E flat:

Example 23

A very concentrated and especially interesting example of the same principle then appears at the very end of the *Grave*. Here a slightly varied version of the concluding motif is formed by the last two notes of the *Grave* plus the first note of the *Allegro*. Let us compare the original motif and the new, varied version of it:

Example 24

The difference is that the first part of the new variant is formed by a major sixth, A flat to C flat (the C flat notated for orthographic reasons as B natural), which is the *prime cell* in inversion. This sixth, however, represents at the same time a part of the new variant of the *concluding motif*. Thus we see here the closest imaginable union of the basic shapes of the *Pathétique*: prime cell and concluding motif merged into three notes.

6. MOTIFS AFFECT MODULATION AND HARMONY

This analysis has been dealing with motifs as the structural forces from which a musical composition is built. However, we all know that in our concept of musical structure, harmonies and harmonic relations also play an integral part.

Now in this sphere of harmonies and harmonization the compositional phenomenon of so-called *modulation* is an important feature. Nevertheless, hardly any directions are to be found, in the various treatises on harmony now current, for determining to which key and for what duration a modulation should be made. Or, as one musician has put it: modulations are in their extent and goals as uncertain as life itself, where no rule can be given as to when and where and how far to travel.

However, the alleged indeterminacy of modulation changes immediately in the light of thematic structure: the works of our great composers clearly reveal *that their modulations are, almost invariably, affected by their thematic lines*. This is demonstrated convincingly in bar 6:

Example 25

With the intention of uttering his prime motif again and again, the composer is almost forcibly led from the G at the end of the first of these two phrases to the shape G, A, B flat, A—that is to an involved modulation. Once he has made the decision, it is, of course, his skill in harmonization that makes this procedure appear as an organic phenomenon, by harmonizing the preceding phrase with the chord of the diminished seventh. And having then reached the last A, he continues, driven by the same 'thematic intention': until he achieves, again through an effective harmonization, the natural return to C minor.

Even the very first bar of the sonata, in its bass-line, furnishes an example of a somewhat similar principle. The bass leaps from C to F sharp (see Example 7). The usual textbook commentary would simply read: the tonic proceeds to the chord of the diminished seventh of the dominant. Very well—but is anything explained by this term? An unusual fact does not become clearer by having a label given to it. Why *this* harmony, and for that matter, why this form—that is, a leap of an augmented fourth, which in Beethoven's time, especially for an opening bar, would certainly appear rather inorganic and rough?

The simple answer is that the motif C, F sharp, G—the concluding motif—was intended to appear.

7. THE ARCHITECTURAL IDEA OF THE *GRAVE* INTRODUCTION

Drawing a summary of the structural scheme of the *Grave*, we may divide it into three parts: the first part (bars 1–5) corresponding to a kind of exposition, the second part (bar 5 to the first part of bar 10) expressing a kind of development, the third part (second half of bar 10) forming a finishing cadence. The motivic structure of these three parts may be charted as follows:

First part: Series of prime motifs plus concluding motif.
Second part: Series of different prime motivic shapes plus series of concluding motifs.
Third part: Prime motif (major inversion) plus concluding motif shaped through prime motivic material.

The logic and symmetry are startling. Going beyond the technical aspect of the structure, however, some questions may be raised. For we realize, of course, that the *Grave*, though shaped into definite periods, has not developed any strict theme, but proceeds in a more or less toccata-like way. Thus it may be asked whether or not there is any deeper architectural idea, according to which the *Grave* is formed, or in other words, whether there is a relationship, and if so of what nature, between the *Grave* and the following sections.

The answer is that there *is* such an underlying architectural idea, and one of great significance. In fact, the *Grave* was formed as a model for the entire work. To function as an outline for the structural source of the first movement specifically, and as a structural source for the whole sonata in general, is its innermost architectural idea. It indicates what the later sections declare. The *Grave*, like all slow introductions in the symphonies of Haydn, Beethoven, Brahms, etc., or the toccatas and preludes of Bach, symbolizes the *improvisational stage of a composition at the moment of its creation*. In these cases, the following allegro or fugue represents *the organized result* of that former quasi-instinctive activity. During the *Grave* one constantly has the feeling that the composer is searching for something. Searching for what? In the frame of this analysis the answer would be 'for a theme'. And this statement is meant not only as an allegory, but as a description much closer to Beethoven's magic reality than might be thought.

3

The Section of the First *Allegro* Theme

1. PIERCING THE STRUCTURAL SURFACE

TURNING from the *Grave* to the *Allegro*, we enter a decisive stage in our analysis. It soon becomes clear that the motivic consistency found to such a degree in the *Grave*, continues beyond it, so that the *Grave* and the *Allegro*, to state this in somewhat summary fashion, are two different manifestations of one basic idea and substance.

In examining the first theme of the *Allegro*, it may at first glance appear that the whole picture has now changed; that is, that the phenomenon of structural continuity in the *Grave*, based on those few motivic fundamentals, has drawn to a close, so that a new structural basis has to be established.

However, upon going deeper into the musical substance, one discovers that there is not only a kind of remote recollection of the *Grave*, or an affinity to it, but that the *Allegro*, indeed, represents an intentional repetition of the shapes and phrases of the *Grave*, *a reflection of its innermost idea*, though different in disposition and character.

Let us first examine the melodic shape of the first two bars of the *Allegro* theme (Example 27). Each bar contains the prime cell, just as in the *Grave*. Moreover, it is exactly the same series, the same melodic-harmonic succession: one cell in C plus one cell in F—the only difference being that the first C minor cell of the *Grave* is in the *Allegro* changed to major.*

---

* This difference is probably the main reason why the analogy between the *Grave* and the *Allegro* has seemingly never been discovered. However, this alteration from minor to major, so common in many musical utterances, is from a structural aspect quite irrelevant. Beethoven needed it in this first *Allegro* bar simply to make the line more fluid. C to E flat (instead of E natural) would, as a link to the following F, have sounded unnecessarily rough. Besides, in order to maintain the original prime-cell idea, it was sufficient to return in the third bar to the minor, which, moreover, gave Beethoven the opportunity to include that

Example 27

However, in the second bar of the *Allegro* theme the prime motif is extended by a few more notes, as follows:

Example 28

But they too, if we look more closely, emerge as a familiar element, namely, the concluding motif, A flat, D, E flat. For reduced from its pianistic surface to its structural essence the line has to be read as follows:

Example 29

Thus a kind of structural miracle unfolds before us. The opening of the *Allegro* theme turns out to be a clear repetition of the opening period of the *Grave*, compressed by means of an accelerated tempo into two bars:

Example 30

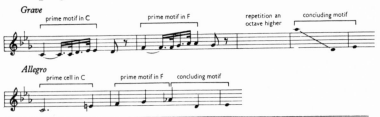

wonderful, abrupt change from minor to major in his line:

Example 26

a change which, in the course of the work, turns out to be a motif in itself.

Through this compression into two bars, however, the repetition of the first phrases of the *Grave*, an octave higher, could not be achieved in the *Allegro* within the opening shape itself. Nevertheless, this feature is not forgotten in the *Allegro*: indeed, as we have seen, the composer repeats the first two bars an octave higher. He repeats them as they are, although they have now an expanded thematic meaning in the *Allegro*, as they also include the concluding motif as well.

In the *Grave*, after the repetition of the first two bars an octave higher, the 'descending passage' concludes the period. And to perfect the analogy, again the same idea appears in the *Allegro*, although here the 'passage', in order to achieve the rhythmical symmetry of the period, had to be extended over four full bars and resolved into a strictly accentuated line or, shall we say, into a theme (see Example 33, bars 5–9).

2. A 'RESTORED' SCORE OF BEETHOVEN

A still more thorough, and indeed amazing picture will become apparent, once we unravel the compact mass of the theme into its single voices. It is worthwhile studying the following example note by note, especially since it must be realized that no note has been changed; the original content has been simply transferred from its pianistic compression to the transparency of an open score:

Example 31

In examining these shapes let us begin with the bass, which is again a replica of the *Grave* theme, this time prolonged in a wide arc. First a prime motif in C rises from a sustained C, then a prime motif in F follows, then finally a concluding motif (in inversion) finishes the period.

This is a startling fact. The *Grave* model, which was repeated in the soprano of the *Allegro* theme, can now be identified also as the definite shape of the bass. And incidentally, this example furnishes an instructive illustration of how in the thematic process, structural strictness and freedom are combined. The old motivic idea is preserved literally—yet the phrasing is changed—the first note, the C, being extended over four full bars (through note-repetition) to fit the present requirements.

In the tenor part the same basic phenomenon confronts us. Here, however, *all* the motifs appear as inversions. Also, a further interesting feature is included—the prime motif in F and the concluding motif are interwoven into one:

Example 32

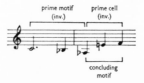

Thus the motivic course of this first shape in the tenor reads: prime motif (inversion) (C, B flat, A flat) then prime motif in F (A flat to F) plus concluding motif (A flat, E, F)—the two latter motifs being of course interwoven. And by the way, just as in the *Grave* and in the soprano part of the *Allegro*, the following two bars are a repetition an octave higher.

In reviewing the features just described, we see the *Grave* model clearly mirrored in the entire bass line of the *Allegro* theme, and also in the first half of all three upper voices, the soprano, the alto and the tenor. Thus only the second half of the upper voices, expressing the 'descending passage', remains to be considered. In this respect the brackets in Example 31 may suffice to demonstrate the motivic detail, which, of course, also consists of the familiar elements. Apart from this detail, however, a *contour* sounds through, disclosing the concluding motif as the melodic kernel of the second half of the theme, as is shown in the following outline:

Example 33

To sum up, we experience an amazing structural spectacle rising out of the *Allegro* theme. First, its opening bars turn out to be an accelerated replica of the *Grave* theme (see Example 30), and the reader is urged to accept this not only as a theoretical fact, but to comprehend its full musical reality, indeed, to *hear* it. Then these two bars, mirroring the *Grave* theme, are used as the core of the *Allegro*, from which the whole theme is developed into a further, higher analogy to the *Grave*, according to the following comparative chart:

Bar 1, *Grave* and *Allegro*: Prime motif in C.

Bar 2, *Grave* and *Allegro*: Prime motif in F.

Bars 3 and 4, *Grave* and *Allegro*: Repetition of the first two bars an octave higher.

End of bar 4, *Grave*; bars 5–8, *Allegro*: Descending passage, expressing the concluding motif.

3. RHYTHM AS A MOTIF

It is not only the melodic–harmonic idea of the *Grave* that is repeated in the *Allegro*. The *rhythm* of the *Grave* also spreads through the new theme. In this respect, too, in spite of the change in character, the essence remains the same.

Let us again recall the rhythm of the *Grave*:

By accelerating the tempo, the dots can easily be lost, and the rhythm of the *Allegro* theme results:

Example 34

In this rhythmical analogy, therefore, two and a half bars of the *Allegro* correspond to only half a bar of the *Grave*. Since, however, as just described, there is also a melodic–harmonic analogy, whereby for instance the first bar of the *Allegro* corresponds to the first of the *Grave*, we realize how a manifold analogy is working here *simultaneously*; rhythmic and melodic motifs converge, even overlap, in one significant phenomenon.*

4. COMPOSING—BUILDING MOTIFS

After the theme has been repeated, this time concluding in a half close, a small group follows. It is rather a simple group, but because of its simplicity, it furnishes an excellent opportunity of making the idea of thematic structure visible in utter transparency.

The group follows, as said, after the theme has been concluded. Now in the course of building a musical work, this is an interesting, exciting moment for the composer. Because, with the conclusion of one thought he has to grope for a new one and he may be in doubt as to whether his inventive fantasy will be able to find it. Thus we may try, at this point, to look into Beethoven's inner workshop, as it were. His ever-flowing fantasy certainly manages to find the 'new thought'. Yet let us look at these bars more closely:

Example 35

[* Réti might perhaps have pointed out that the rhythm of the first *Allegro* theme has actually *been* evolved, in the very way he indicates, during the *Grave* itself (see his own comment on the shifting of rhythm and accent in bar 6 of the *Grave*, in section 4 of the previous chapter). The example here is mine.—ED.]

36

This is indeed a prime cell (inversion in the major) plus finishing motif, followed by a descending passage, which is formed by two successive concluding motifs.

Now, before proceeding further, let us become aware of the full phenomenon here involved—become not just 'theoretically' aware of it, but conscious of it as a musical reality. The melodic extract of the *Grave* theme is seen in Example 36(a) while the extract of the present group is shown in Example 36(b).

Example 36

In this comparison we see clearly the difference in the two shapings—for, of course, there *are* differences; no real composition could grow, were its design merely a constant repetition of the same phrases. But we also see the identity of the inner kernels. The differences are that the prime cell appears in the *Allegro* group in inversion, while the second prime cell utterance of the *Grave* is omitted in the *Allegro*; and on the other hand the concluding motif, which in the *Grave* appears only once, is in the *Allegro* increased to a series of two. Yet the similarity in the structural plan of both shapings is too striking to be questioned.

One might say, however, that all this referred only to the soprano part, during which a bass line was of course also sounding. Let us look at this too: again and again it spells the same pattern—prime motif plus concluding motif. This becomes apparent in the following extract:

Example 37

5. AN INCONSPICUOUS BASS-LINE

The remaining portion of this section reveals an uninterrupted flow of interwoven motifs, whereby all our familiar elements are constantly merged into one another. Looking at the detail, we first recognize a series of overlapping concluding motifs, while at the same time prime cells are expressed through the *corner contours*:*

Example 38

until finally the line resolves into a series of interwoven concluding and finishing motifs:

Example 39

During all this, a long bass-line rises (bars 35–49).† There is, in customary analytical comment, little structural content attributed to such conventional bass tremolo, which would usually be explained as a dominant pedal, moving to B flat. However, it soon becomes clear that this inconspicuous bass-line is a much extended prime motif in its chromatic version.

Example 40

[* For Réti's use of the words 'corner' and 'contour', see next chapter, section 2.—Ed.]

[† The method of bar-numbering differs in different editions of the Sonata. Réti follows the numbering which counts straight through from the first bar of the *Grave* to the end of the movement, the two first-time bars at the end of the *Allegro* exposition being taken as 131–132, and the two second-time bars as 133–134.—Ed.]

4

The Section of the Second *Allegro* Theme

1. THE MELODIC MOTIF

ALREADY on the alert from our preceding analysis, we quickly recognize our familiar motifs as basic elements also in the second theme. Or to state this more precisely: the structural idea of the *Grave*, the prime source from which the whole stream of the *Pathétique* springs, is mirrored clearly in the section of the second *Allegro* theme.

The first group of this theme reads:

Example 41

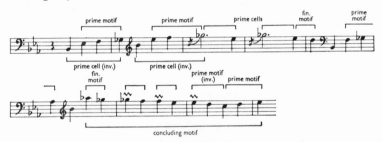

Its essence is once again the prime cell (in contrary motion) plus the finishing motif—that is, the image of the sonata's opening bar, followed by the concluding motif (A flat, D, E flat, just as in the *Grave* theme). This concluding motif clearly sounds as the melodic contour of the second half of the above group.*

Apart from this, however, another feature attracts our attention, namely bars 5 and 6 of the theme, where, for the first time since the beginning of the sonata, a new shape, not identified in our motivic list, emerges. It is the ascending seventh, B flat to A flat:

[* Also present in bars 6–7 of Example 41, as Réti himself indicates in Example 53b, is a 'prime motif' (inverted)—A flat, G flat, F.—ED.]

39

Example 42

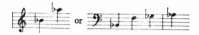

True, this seventh could, if connected with the following note, the G flat, be regarded as a part of an altered version of the concluding motif:

Example 43

and this is exactly the way in which a new feature was usually introduced by Beethoven, that is as a part or a variant of an already familiar element. Yet through its melodic emphasis, and moreover through its repeated application in the later course of the work, this seventh is lifted to the definite role of a motif in itself. Indeed, Beethoven would not have been Beethoven had he sounded such an ear-catching shape just as a single casual utterance without any structural consequence. In fact, this little phrase assumes a very significant function in the *Pathétique*. We may call it the *melodic motif*, since the composer usually inserts it when desirous of a specific melodic intensity.

2. THE CORNER INTERVAL

The 'melodic motif' has emerged here for the first time as a concrete phrase. However, in a more indirect, somewhat hidden form, it was present in the sonata from the beginning. Looking once again at the opening period of the *Grave* (Example 4), we discover the same ascending seventh to be the very interval which spans the melodic line from C in bar 1 to the B flat in bar 4. Such an interval spanning the lowest and the highest note of a group will henceforth be referred to as a 'corner interval', as it encompasses the corner notes of a group.*

It is clear that in some of his works, Beethoven established such motivic corner intervals as additional structural features, and the *Pathétique* belongs to this class. Indeed, an examination reveals that all

---

* In this sonata, the seventh as a corner interval is the form in which the 'melodic motif' appears in wider shape—or in other words, the melodic motif in contour forms the corner interval of the seventh. This should be kept in mind throughout the following deductions, whenever the terms 'corner interval' and 'melodic motif' are used, in order to avoid any misunderstanding of the two conceptions.

the groups of the sonata, throughout all the movements, show only two forms of corner interval: the *seventh* (or its inversion the *ninth*) and the *octave*. It seems that, in general, the octave was chosen for the more concisely and rhythmically shaped groups, whereas the seventh and the ninth were chosen for the freer and more transitory ones.

Accordingly, we list, in the part of the sonata analysed so far, the following corner intervals:

The Grave
    Opening period (bars 1–4): The seventh (C to B flat).
    Following part of the *Grave* (5–10): The ninth (E flat to F).
The section of the first Allegro theme
    Theme (bars 11–18 and 19–26): The octave (C to C).
    Bridges (27–30 and 31–34): The ninth (F sharp to G).
    Bridging group of three bars (35–37): Without corner interval of
        seventh or ninth.
    Last group repeated (38–41): The seventh (E flat to D flat).
    Same group repeated again (42–45): The seventh (F to E flat).
    Finishing group (45–50): The ninth (A to B flat).

In the section of the second *Allegro* theme, the corner intervals are constantly formed by the seventh, for instance:

    First group (51–59): B flat to A flat.
    Second group (59–67): A flat to G flat.

3. PRIME MOTIF, VARIED VERSION

As described above, prime cells were found to be the foremost structural particles of the second theme. However, since this section is built in harmonic units of four bars each, let us try to connect these units in order to see whether an overall shape, a contour, may emerge.

Let us examine bars 51–70 in the text. By contracting each four bars of the line into one unit, the following scheme appears:

Example 44

What does this shaping express? It is again the prime motif which thus appears as the model according to which the second *Allegro* theme is shaped. However, it is the prime motif in a somewhat varied version. The original motif (in contrary motion) would read: A flat, G flat, F. But here it reads, beginning with the middle note: G flat, A flat, G flat, F.

Some scepticism may arise with regard to the above explanation. One might ask whether the classification of this phrase as a version of the prime motif is based on reality, or is merely an artificial analytical conjecture—in other words, whether the similarity really reflects a structural intention of the composer or is simply an incidental feature. However, it is Beethoven himself who furnishes the answer. For, this same varied version—*literally* the same—appears also as a motif in the detail of the sonata at this very moment. It is the mordent in bar 57 and the following bars, reading:

Example 45

In view of this, there can no longer be any doubt. This simultaneous appearance of the same particular shape, both in detail and as an overall contour, is certainly more than a casual coincidence.*

Moreover, it seems we have reached a point where varied versions develop in the course of the work. For not only varied versions of the prime motif emerge, but bars 75 and 79 present the concluding motif in analogously varied shapes:

Example 46

and these, by the way, are interwoven with a kind of inversion of the prime motif in contrary motion, as can be seen.

---

* Incidentally, attention may be directed to the fact, so characteristic of Beethoven's way of all-permeating structural thinking, that his *ornaments* never represent mere embellishments, but always contain some motivic substance, just as in the case above. There is hardly any acciaccatura, turn, mordent or trill in his music which does not conform to some structural idea. The reason for notating these motifs as ornaments is that in this way the composer is able to make *several thematic lines visible simultaneously*, which might otherwise escape the reader's or the performer's attention. In Example 41 the basic line shows finishing motifs to which the mordents are added as prime motivic shapes. The *Rondo* is full of similar instances.

4. EFFECT OF ORIGINAL PITCH

In order to complete the analysis of this section, we continue our extraction of its structure by connecting its harmonic units.

The first group, as just demonstrated, expressed the prime motif in its varied version. Now, the following part (bars 71–82) expresses the prime motif also, with two concluding motifs interpolated. The extract of these bars produces the following shape:

Example 47

However, we should not forget the bass line of this section (bars 51–75). It reveals an inversion of the concluding motif in a particularly long shape:

Example 48

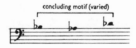

After this, the remainder of the bass is formed by a series of prime motifs and concluding motifs (bars 75–90).

Throughout this whole section the new motif, the 'melodic' seventh, rises five times in the soprano part. The climax is reached in bar 80, reading:

Example 49

Here the motif appears *at the same pitch* as in its original appearance, where it was the corner interval of the sonata's opening period, C to B flat.

Such 'original pitch'★ represents a significant phenomenon in musical architecture. For it is only natural that composers try to have their motifs sound, when possible, at one pitch at decisive points of their compositions. Here too, both the melodic motif and the concluding

★ *The Thematic Process of Music*, p. 53.

motif appear at their original pitch at the very moment when the climax is reached; whereafter the concluding motif sounds twice, transposed, bringing the section to a close.

Example 50

The last accentuated note of this line is C (with an annexed B flat as a finishing motif, bar 87), while the first melodic note of the next section is an E flat:

Example 51

Thus the prime cell sounds here, even in this extraordinary form of a link between two different sections. Moreover, the link is a prime cell at *original pitch*.

5

Third *Allegro* Section and Repetition of First *Allegro* Theme

1. CONCEPT OF A THEMATIC PATTERN

A N examination of the third *Allegro* section may enrich our idea of motivic technique with some new principles. *For at this point it will have become clear that thematic connections account not only for the structural detail of a work but also for its larger shaping and gradually even for its widest architectural plan.*★

Thematically, as indicated at the end of the foregoing chapter, this third section begins in the last bars of the second section with the note C, which forms the prime cell as a kind of *auftakt* to the E flat. We may thus draw up the motivic scheme of the theme of the third section as follows:

Example 52

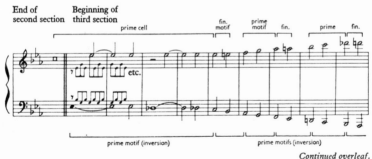

Continued overleaf.

★ The expressions structure and architecture, so often used throughout this analysis, refer to two related yet different concepts (perhaps somewhat comparable to the difference between tactics and strategy in the military sphere). 'Structure' embraces all the detailed features through which the course of a composition is brought about, while 'architecture' points to that larger plan through which its higher unity which we call 'form' is shaped. Thus architecture comes into existence through structure, but structure as such does not cover the whole sphere of those partly undefined concepts which are included in architecture.

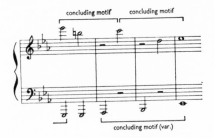

Both lines of this example are formed through a series of prime motifs plus concluding motifs. This in itself may be regarded as self-evident. The truly significant realization, however, arises from comparing *all* the thematic sections analysed so far. For, in doing so, it becomes apparent that these themes are not only built from the same motivic substance but, indeed, from one basic pattern.

The idea of a *thematic pattern*, which now may be introduced into the analysis, is a structural concept of the highest importance. If the cells and motifs can be regarded as bricks of a work's structure, then the 'patterns' are its larger units. Or, more specifically, *the patterns are the motivic ideas of the themes*. The fact that our classical composers apply such unifying patterns, according to which the different themes and groups of a work are shaped, lifts thematic technique to a higher level and makes it a true form-building force in music.

Let us see how one thematic pattern is at work in the *Pathétique*. The pattern, underlying the opening group of the *Grave*, was, as we may recall:

> *Prime motif plus finishing motif in C.*
> *Prime motif plus finishing motif in F.*
> Finally, *concluding motif.*

Now, by looking at the themes of the *Allegro* one by one, we become aware that all the thematic groups of the *Allegro* are built from this basic pattern.

Example 53

(a) First *Allegro* theme:

46

(b) Second *Allegro* theme:

(c) Third *Allegro* theme:

Thus, the identical pattern of all these themes cannot be questioned. The multiplicity of the work, however, is brought about through the specific variants in which this basic pattern appears in the different sections.

In the second theme, for instance, which is in E flat, the prime cell (inversion) naturally has also to sound in E flat, which, however, is very close to C minor. As another variant the prime cell in F and the concluding motif are in this same section interwoven into one.

In the third theme, after the prime motifs in C and F, a third one in B flat is interpolated (omitted in the example) and the end of this theme is shaped as a series of two consecutive concluding motifs instead of a single one.

All these are variants—the very variants through which the phenomenon which we call composition is achieved. For composing means varying; and a work, as we have said, cannot be built as a mere literal repetition of the same shapes. Yet in essence, the *pattern* remains the same.

And the pattern is no less recognizable even in the bridging groups, that is the groups between the themes:

Example 54

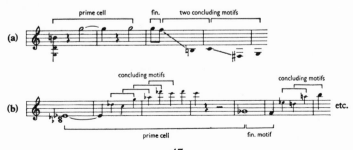

47

In the latter interesting combination, the prime motif plus finishing motif forms the inner contour, while interwoven concluding motifs appear as figurations.

Similarly, the second part of the *Grave* consists of a series of prime motifs and finishing motifs (partly, as described earlier, in different accentuation or in chromatic versions), followed by two concluding motifs (bars 5–10). And even the very end of the *Grave* spells the same idea again:

Example 55

2. A HUGE ARCHITECTURAL IDEA

Besides the phenomena just described, another development takes shape, through which the final architectural role of the *Grave* becomes clear. For by comparing the sections of the *Grave* with the sections of the *Allegro*, a startling analogy arises. Let us divide the *Grave* and the exposition of the *Allegro* into four sectional parts. The following chart will show how each section of the *Grave* is clearly mirrored in the corresponding section of the *Allegro*:

Example 56

These are facts from which there is no escape. Just as the four parts expressing the pattern follow each other in the *Grave*, so, in precisely the same order, are the corresponding parts mirrored in the *Allegro*. Thus the innermost idea of the *Grave* manifests itself not as a casual 'introduction' but as an improvised draft of the *Allegro*, outlining the plan of the work to be.

3. SOME ACCENTUATED CHORDS

Before proceeding further, we may note the corner intervals. The corner interval in the first period of the third thematic section (bars 89–100) is the octave, E flat to E flat; in the repetition of this group (101–112) the ninth, E flat to F. In the following group (113–116), and also in its repetition (bars 117–120) the seventh, G to F, is heard.

With this last group, the virtual end of the exposition has been reached, and the first theme is again given out, now *forte* and transposed into the traditional relative major, E flat.

Then, before proceeding to the repetition or to the development, a series of accentuated chords follows, accompanied by a bass line of prime motifs (see Example 70).

What do these outbursts mean? At first thought one might be inclined to classify these chords as merely the usual *fortissimo* effects by which a work or a large section of it is so often concluded. Probing more deeply, however, they appear as a musical manifestation of true grandeur, on which one of the principal points of the work's architecture is centred. Yet an analytical explanation of the phenomenon here involved has to be postponed to the end of this movement. Meanwhile, we may turn to the question of a rather strange error which has become customary in the performance of this sonata.

49

4. TRADITION—YET DISTORTION

At the end of the exposition Beethoven notated the usual repetition mark. However, he failed to designate the corresponding mark, either at the beginning of the work, or at any part of the exposition (see Breitkopf und Haertel, *Kritische Gesamtausgabe*).

No doubt owing to the lack of this corresponding mark, performers, left to their own discretion, developed the habit of repeating the *Allegro* only, of omitting the *Grave* from the repetition. And many of the later editions did not hesitate to perpetrate this senseless procedure in print.

Beethoven obviously imagined it as self-evident that the whole of the exposition, including the *Grave* introduction, would be repeated, as long as no mark indicated the contrary. Be this as it may, and even if the error could be traced back to a copyist or one early edition, there remain numerous proofs that it is a plain distortion to put the repetition mark at the beginning of the *Allegro* rather than at the beginning of the *Grave*.

1. Beethoven revealed his architectural design clearly by interpolating a part of the *Grave* before both the development and the coda.

2. Had Beethoven intended to start the repetition from the *Allegro*, then he certainly would not have reintroduced the *Allegro* theme a few bars before the repetition. Such a reintroduction is, it should be realized, in itself a quite rare, indeed a unique case within his sonatas. One can only think that he did *not* intend to return to the *Allegro* immediately, but had decided to interpolate first a repetition of the *Grave*. For every grain of architectural feeling indicates that the re-entrance of the theme, *piano*, so soon after it has been heard in a triumphant *forte*, must appear as a feeble anticlimax.

3. Besides, this abrupt change from the *fortissimo* bar before the repetition to the *piano* of the *Allegro* theme would prove, even from a purely pianistic point of view, extremely awkward in performance. To overcome this, most performers find it necessary to include a breathing space between the two bars, which, however, represents a definite falsification of the text.

4. Last but not least, there is the matter of motivic continuity. For Beethoven introduced the *Allegro* theme throughout the whole movement from the leading note to the tonic (in most cases B natural to C). Let us look at these occurrences:

Example 57

In the latter case, for instance, how easy, how almost logical it would have been to drop from the upper D to the lower D. However, Beethoven chose the B, because he wanted this as a motivic note.

Finally there is one more instance—bars 196–197, the point of re-capitulation:

Example 58

Viewed superficially, these bars would seem to negate our contention. For here indeed, the last *printed* note before the recapitulation of the theme is not B, but D. However, looking from the surface to the structural essence, the picture appears somewhat differently. The motivic extract of the whole group (bars 189–197) reads as follows:

Example 59

which means an uninterrupted series of prime cells plus the concluding motif, a structural shape which cannot be broken. Thus the annexed notes in the last bar before the re-entrance of the theme merely form a swirling passage down to the bass, and the last *real* note, that is the last structural note before the C of the theme, is B.

6

Development and Recapitulation

1. REAL AND CLASSROOM MODULATION

THE development begins with an echo of the *Grave* reduced to four bars. Two of these bars are a literal transposition of the first part of the *Grave* to G minor. The remainder forms a modulation to E minor.

Such a modulation usually appears in theoretical exercises as a procedure explained through more or less intricate relations between harmonies. In contrast, how natural is modulation in the living composition. The reason for this, as already described on a previous occasion, is that in the living composition a modulation is not conceived as an abstract phenomenon connecting various keys, but as an expression of a *thematic course*.

The first two bars of the *Grave* interpolation contain the motif in its usual shape. In the next bar, however, the composer changes the last particle, the finishing motif, to its contrary motion, leading the E flat (D sharp) to E natural instead of to D. That is all. And the chord so reached, the 6/4 of E minor, is simply followed by the usual cadence, in order both to confirm the new key and to express the concluding motif— or more precisely—to express an interesting series of motifs interwoven in the concluding motif. Incidentally, the corner interval of this E minor group is the ninth, D sharp to E.

2. ALL SECTIONS COMBINE

In the following *Allegro* part of the development, the whole thematic material of the preceding exposition is merged.

Example 60

The first two bars echo a part of the first *Allegro* section. The following bars combine two sections in one: in their rhythmic shape, the second *Allegro* section; and in their melodic line, the *Grave*.

And by the way, this same *Grave* shape (prime motif plus finishing motif) is shown a few bars later in an interesting extension:

Example 61

during which the bass is rising in the familiar interwoven figures of the finishing and concluding motifs.

Then the line descends as an uninterrupted series of finishing motifs interwoven with prime motifs, thus somewhat mirroring the third *Allegro* section in contrary motion (cf. Example 52):

Example 62

However, the transparency and simplicity of the underlying musical idea of this development soon becomes fully apparent, once we turn to its thematic essence. For by omitting the interwoven figurations of finishing and concluding motifs, and by drawing merely the thematic contour, this whole long and rather complex shaping can be reduced to one structural unit.

Example 63

3. ARCHITECTURAL PILLARS

Interrupting our structural examination of the single groups for a few moments, we may shift our analysis to a wider sphere, and try to discover thematic patterns as working forces even in the largest thinkable proportions.

In the beginning of the analysis the idea was put forward of a relationship existing between the opening period of the *Grave* and the following one, through their respective keys. C to E flat forms a large expression of the prime cell. Analogously, however, we may recognize the whole of the exposition of the *Allegro*, which progresses from C to E flat, as a prime cell with still larger proportions.

Then, after the exposition, a reduced replica of the *Grave* is interpolated, starting from G minor. Thus another expression of the cell is spelled, through this key relationship E flat to G. And this architectural chain of cells is continued, since the following *Allegro* part of the development is in E minor. Through this the relationship between the two sections becomes G to E natural, that is the prime cell in inversion.

Now, however, we may pause to consider this E natural for a moment. It does seem rather unusual to have the development of a C minor sonata, moreover one from Beethoven's early period, moving towards E natural. We demonstrated earlier how smoothly and simply, through a 'thematic modulation', the key of E natural was reached. But this referred only to the technical side of the modulation rather than to the wider question of why the composer chose E natural for his development at all.

The answer may emerge from continued examination of the key relationships of the architectural parts of the sonata. For in relation to the basic C, this E natural is again the prime cell in the major. And linked to the prime cell in the minor, as formed through the exposition, the whole design thus spells that *alteration of the cell from minor to major* which we recognised from the beginning as a motivic feature in itself. Here this change appears to be almost as abrupt as its occurrence in miniature in the opening of the *Allegro*:

Example 64

In addition, the development itself, finally flowing on to a pedal of G, forms a large shape of the (transposed) cell, E to G. Now we may try to find out how this prime cell, this architectural progression from E to G, is actually brought about. The following is the extract of the development's bass-line in contour, through which this whole shape is formed:

Example 65

It turns out to be a large concluding motif in a kind of chromatic version.

As a supplement to this, another phenomenon which emerged in the *Grave* may now be pointed out—its bass-line. The only reason for having postponed its description to this late moment instead of including it in the structural picture of the *Grave* itself is that it would hardly have been understandable at that early stage of the analysis. Now, however, it will be easily recognized as the fundamental pattern of the *Grave*: the prime cell expressed through the harmonic relationship between the first and second periods, plus the concluding motif. The concluding motif is formed by the descent of the bass-line from the E flat to its lowest corner, the F sharp, in order to turn back to the G, as the last 'pillar note' of the bass. See the bass-line of Example 14—in contour the line reads:

Example 66

The architectural scheme of the whole movement may now be easily drawn. It appears, as seen in the following chart, as an amazing *expression of the basic motifs* of the work, formed through these giant harmonic–melodic arcs:

Example 67

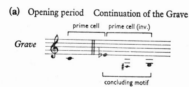

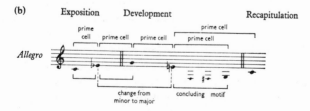

4. A FOURFOLD REPETITION

Returning to the development of the *Allegro*, we have now arrived at two bars to which our attention is directed immediately, since they are repeated within a small space no less than four times:

Example 68

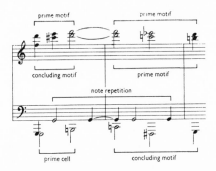

It may be worth while examining their motivic elements, indicated above by brackets, voice by voice. They form a delicate fretwork of motivic art. Incidentally, the shape of these two bars was already heard in the foregoing group, as can be seen by resolving its figuration into a series of chords:*

Example 69

However, apart from the interesting detail involved, these two bars form a particular point of expression. They are shaped as a series of two prime motifs (up and down), a fact which in itself, of course, is no novelty. But the particular phenomenon here is the emphatic form in which these prime motifs are spelled. Because after the complex combinations, inversions, etc., of the preceding groups, we now hear the motifs again as, so to speak, a melodic manifestation. One has the impression that the composer at last, after many detours, wished to utter his basic thought directly. So filled does he seem with this desire that he repeats these two bars no less than four times, only once interrupted through a short reiteration of the preceding group. Were a student to introduce a fourfold repetition of two small bars like these in his assignment, the teacher would—and rightly so—advise him to cancel at least one of them. Here, however, as a motivic climax in the architecture of the *Allegro*, the repetition forms an utterance of extraordinary intensity.

With these bars the development is virtually at its end, as any new thought would appear to be but a lessening. What follows is merely a bridge (Example 59)—a chain of prime cells (plus the concluding motif)

[* Also, compare Examples 68 and 69 with Examples 44 and 45.—ED.]

—to the recapitulation. The B as the last motivic note of this group, now appears, in the light of the wider connections, all the more founded.

5. THE PRIME CELL SOUNDS

The ensuing recapitulation represents, as classical recapitulations do, a repetition of the exposition, but modulating differently, of course; that is, finally progressing to the tonic key, C minor, instead of the relative major. Yet Beethoven's ever-flowing inspiration produces quite a number of small but very interesting variations. These are especially interesting from the point of view of this analysis, since the changes are obviously caused by the composer's desire to include different combinations of motifs and still express the same musical idea. But since the motivic elements in these variations are by now familiar to us, their discovery can be left to the reader.

At the end of the recapitulation the same series of accentuated chords confronts us as at the end of the exposition—this time, of course, in C minor.

As suggested previously, these chords, at first glance, might appear as the usual concluding *fortissimo*, without much importance as a musical utterance. In reality, however, the very core of the first movement's dramatic idea is centred in these bars. In order to understand their true significance, we have to compare the two occurrences, the first in the exposition and the second in the recapitulation:

Example 70

(a) Exposition

This is the first appearance. What actually happens here? The composer, after having reached the end of the exposition, sees himself at the peak of an emotional and structural climax. Emotion should induce him to a final utteranc of the utmost intensity. As regards structure, however, he is at a kind of dead-end. Structurally, this utterance could again—as all utterances of the sonata—only be formed by a shape which is in some way derived from the prime cell. But how is one to form a prime cell, reading C to E flat, from E flat as a starting point? (A new prime cell shape—one transposed from E flat to G flat, for instance—would appear out of the question at this point, of course: it would simply destroy the whole architectural design of the exposition, which was formed as a huge prime cell at its original pitch, C to E flat.)

Therefore, locked in the sphere of E flat, from whence there is no way out, the composer hammers his chord four times in an ever growing *forte*. Then he does all that he can do, in order at least to approach the expression of an intensified prime cell; namely, he changes the chord from

Example 71

He thus spells the cell in solid form rather than in a melodic line, for the melodic line must remain immovably on E flat. Yet all this effort brings no real solution—at least none to the emotional problem involved.

Finally, the line falls back (through the prime cell shape in contrary motion) to the initial C, the tonic:

Example 72

and *the whole course of the work must be attempted again.* This renewed attempt is the inner sense of the repetition and the following development. Or to describe the same phenomenon in other words: in the *Pathétique, the idea of sonata-form itself,* as outlined in the traditional scheme of exposition, development, etc., is miraculously used as an expression of the dramatic content, by means of thematic structure.

Coming back to our accentuated chords, this same group assumes a quite different appearance and meaning in its second occurrence in the recapitulation:

Example 73

Here the climax is reached in C minor; and starting from C, it is not only a possible, but almost a self-evident, procedure to form an expression of the prime cell through a leap to E flat. And this is precisely what we see happen in the sonata. The prime cell sounds, no longer as a shaped motif. The naked cell is thrown out in a tremendous *fortissimo*, followed by—nothing; or to be more precise, a rest. There is not even an attempt to shape the whole series into the usual form of a rounded group or a cadenced period, it appears rather as a naked cry, a musical utterance unheard until Beethoven's time.

With this, all that the composer had to say has been said—the movement is at its end. What follows is only a recollection of things past: first a few bars of the *Grave*, then the beginning of the *Allegro*, and finally a varied repetition of the prime cell's outcry—the story of the whole movement, compressed into a few bars.

And to add an outer conclusion to the inner resolution, the concluding motif, in the form of a finishing cadence, is annexed as an ending:

Example 74

That these three annexed bars are meant to belong together, thus forming the concluding motif, is proved by the added bar's rest. For by adding this bar's rest to the three bars forming the concluding motif, the four-bar symmetry, so important at the conclusion of the movement, is now achieved.

This appearance of the concluding motif merely as a finishing cadence brings about still another structural phenomenon which later in the work assumes much significance. The explanation of this will be given in the analysis of the *Rondo*.

7
The *Adagio*

1. ARCHITECTURAL UNITY COMPRISING ALL MOVEMENTS

CAN the close structural connection described in the foregoing analysis be pursued beyond the borders of a single movement? Is there some architectural unity welding together the separate parts of this sonata? That such a unity does exist and is present in most of the greater works of the classical era, is demonstrated at length in *The Thematic Process in Music*.

2. THE SPECIFIC MOTIF OF THE *ADAGIO*

Turning now to the *Adagio* of the *Pathétique*, let us first look at the melodic line in the two opening bars. The shape of these two bars is clearly a mirroring of the first phrase of the *Grave*, expressing the prime cell plus the finishing motif:

Example 75

However, Beethoven has woven the note B flat into the original line. Or rather, he has changed the original ascending second, C to D, to its contrary motion, C to B flat—a variant which, in combination with the slow tempo and rhythm, produces the desired songlike character for the *Adagio*. Moreover, through this variant, the phrase, which is already an expression of the prime cell C to E flat, becomes in addition an expression of the concluding motif (in two interwoven shapes: C, B flat, E flat; and B flat, E flat, D flat).

Thus we recognize our basic combination—prime cell plus finishing motif plus concluding motif—as the structural substance of the *Adagio* also, even in these first two bars.

Now let us proceed to the next two bars, the melodic line of which reads as follows:

Example 76

This phrase would appear to represent the prime cell. Yet its melodic essence is obviously neither the prime cell nor the concluding motif, but something else. Looking at it more closely, we discover that this shape is not unknown to us. It is, indeed, the ascending seventh—the melodic motif from the first movement; and moreover at its original pitch—that is the pitch expressed through the corner interval of the opening period of the *Grave*. Apart from its role as a 'corner interval', we may recall that this melodic motif emerged as a little shape in the second section of the second *Allegro* theme (Example 43).

Here, however, in the *Adagio*, it is designed to become one of the specific motivic features. In each of the themes of the second movement we find the melodic seventh as a decisive part of its structure. In these themes, it appears either in its original form as an *ascending* seventh (or in inversion as a ninth), or sometimes *descending*, in contrary motion, but always with the special melodic emphasis so appropriate to the 'melodic' character of an *Adagio*.

Once having understood this, we may also realize how the B flat, the variant from the first bar of the *Adagio*, assumes an even more meaningful role. For, now the descending step C to B flat appears not only as the contrary motion of C to D, but also as the inversion of the melodic motif (at its original pitch).

Thus, Beethoven managed to include all the structural bricks of the *Grave* in the first two bars of the *Adagio*, namely the prime cell, the finishing motif, the concluding motif and the melodic motif, as well as a new feature which will be described in the following.

3. FOURTHS AND FIFTHS AS MOTIVIC FEATURES

The melodic variant from the first bar, the B flat, produced another interval, a perfect fourth, B flat to E flat. Why is this significant? Because this is virtually the first time in the course of the sonata that a perfect fourth appears as a clear and so to speak autonomous part of the melodic line.

It would be interesting to know how many readers are aware that throughout the whole first movement, perfect fourths (and their inversions, fifths) never emerged as *musical* elements. When appearing at all, these fourths and fifths remained inconspicuous, involuntary particles of other shapes. For instance, bars 35ff. of the first movement reveal this shaping:

Example 77

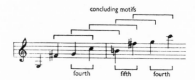

These fourths and fifths, as seen above, are parts of the concluding motifs, and the original diminished fifths are in these cases varied to perfect intervals.

In principle the same thing happens in the *Adagio*. The fourth in question, B flat to E flat, emerges from the concluding motif:

Example 78

And looking at the bass, or at the alto, we see the same spectacle: the fourths and fifths can invariably be recognized as parts of some concluding motifs.

Yet in the *Adagio* these fourths and fifths increase both in number and in melodic intensity, and thus assume more and more of a thematic character. Perhaps they should not yet be termed full motifs, but at any rate motivic features. In this way these motivic fourths and fifths permeate the whole *Adagio* throughout all its sections.

4. THE *ADAGIO* PATTERN

In the first movement, we discovered as one of its most striking architectural phenomena the analogy by which the single sections of the

Allegro were formed as images of corresponding parts of the *Grave*.

Now a still wider analogy becomes apparent. For, the opening period of the *Grave*, the prime source of all the shapes of the first movement, is now revealed as the architectural model for the groups of the *Adagio* as well:

Example 79

Were only one of the structural elements of the *Grave* theme to re-emerge in the *Adagio*, we should perhaps have to accept it as a rather casual coincidence. But the appearance of all three motivic parts (prime cell in C plus prime cell in F plus concluding motif), *moreover in exactly the same succession as in the Grave*, certainly represents too striking a phenomenon not to be recognized as the clear intention of the composer. Thus the fact of the existing analogy can hardly be questioned.

Yet we must avoid any misunderstanding. For it would be quite wrong to assume that this analysis is bent on proving the *Grave* theme and the *Adagio* theme to be identical in pattern. What is claimed is merely a similarity of some parts of their inner structural kernels. Beyond this inner similarity, however, there are some *differences* which are no less visible. In fact the simultaneous existence of similarities and differences touches the heart of the thematic process. Were it not for the inner unity permeating the whole composition, a work, no matter what its other qualities might be, would have to be regarded as a kind of potpourri rather than a real composition; but on the other hand, were it not for the differences, no higher architectural form like a sonata could grow at all, but the work would at best remain a series of repetitions and variations.

In the present specific case, for example, this difference becomes convincingly apparent even in the opening bars. An identical framing of the two shapes is too clear to be doubted. Yet the difference in tempo, rhythm, etc., and especially the alteration of the D of the *Grave* to its contrary motion, the B flat, is of course not just a negligible, accidental nuance, but reflects the decision to change the appearance and character of the *Grave* theme essentially.

The shaping of the second bar of the *Grave* (Example 80(a)) is in the *Adagio* subdued to a contrapuntal role in the bass (Example 80(b)); while the soprano part (Example 80(c)) carries a different phrase, showing the melodic motif which appeared in the first movement in quite another connection. Thus here too the *Grave* idea is still alive, yet a quite different impression on the listener is brought about through added emphasis on the new soprano line. And the concluding motif of the *Grave* theme (Example 80(d)), in its reiteration in the *Adagio*, is extended to a transposed threefold repetition (Example 80(e)).

Example 80

Therefore, the same principle is found to be at work through the whole *Adagio* theme as in the *Grave*—but there are also differences to be seen. These differences not only confer a new musical flavour on the *Adagio*—they even make us recognize a new thematic pattern emerging in this movement, the specific *pattern of the Adagio*.

What is this *Adagio* pattern?

It is, as might be anticipated, the pattern of the first movement, enriched by some additional features. The most significant of these new features has already been outlined. It consists of the inclusion of the melodic motif—which in the first movement appeared merely as a transitory element: in the second thematic section of the *Allegro*, for instance, or in the opening period of the *Grave* (in a more indirect form as a 'corner interval'). This melodic motif, however, now becomes a substantial motivic part of the whole *Adagio*.

A chart of the *Adagio* pattern would therefore read:

1. Prime cell (plus finishing motif) when possible in C and F.
2. Melodic motif (seventh or ninth).
3. Concluding motif.

or in other words, the *Adagio* pattern is a replica of the pattern of the first movement plus an interpolated melodic motif.

One must realize that, in the midst of all the themes of the *Adagio*,

64

each time the line of the theme strives toward its peak, as if by law, a seventh or a ninth (the melodic motif), or a series of them, is interpolated. The themes of the *Adagio*, these wonderful shapes which we must recognize as a great artist's desire to manifest himself in music—in 'song'—are revealed on closer examination to be variants of one structural idea:

Example 81

And now we may look into the themes one by one.

Example 82. *First theme:*

This theme has already been described. The pattern emerges in all clarity, the melodic seventh in bar 3 forms the centre of the first half, the concluding motif appears at the end as a series of three.*

* Bar 4 of this theme produces a little phrase:

Example 83

which in the coda of the *Adagio* is reiterated as an individual motivic shape. We may call it the 'particle', as it strikingly resembles a part of the prime motif in chromatic form from the *Grave*, where it read:

The fact that this same little phrase appears as the beginning of the third *Allegro* section, there reading:

as well as here in the *Adagio*, and especially, as hinted, in its coda, moreover *always at the same pitch*, proves the distinct motivic character of this particle.

Example 84. *Second theme:*

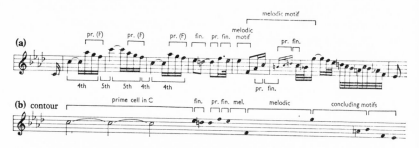

Here the prime cell forms the first half of the theme. The first three bars are melodically centred on C; yet when connected to bar 4, one large prime cell plus finishing motif (C, E flat, D) is expressed (Example 84(b)). While this large prime cell in C is sounded, the prime cell in F also becomes audible through the figurations in the soprano (the interwoven fourths and fifths). Through this the familiar shape, prime cell in C plus prime cell in F, which emerged in the *Grave* as two consecutive bars, appears in this second *Adagio* theme interwoven into one group. After this, one more prime cell plus finishing motif (now transposed) appears in bar 4 of the example above.

Now the point is reached where the melodic motif is interpolated in twofold succession, first as a descending seventh, then as a rising ninth (the ninth formed through prime-motive figurations). In the seventh and the ninth the peak of the melodic emphasis is centred; after which the remainder of the theme is formed by means of a 'descending passage' —which, as might be expected, expresses the concluding motif, or to be exact, two concluding motifs.

Example 85. *Third theme:*

After an introductory *auftakt*, formed characteristically as a perfect fourth, the first bars consist of a prime cell sounded three times plus a finishing motif (a concluding motif is interwoven into the first occurrence). Then the melodic motif is interpolated twice, first in a leap between two bars, as an ascending seventh, A flat to G flat (the G flat is notated as F sharp). From the F sharp the line rises once again in an emphatic seventh to E natural; after which the familiar pair of concluding motifs ends the theme. It is interesting to note that the last seventh, F sharp to E, is here shown to be a combination of two perfect fourths (with fifths interwoven).

Thus, the underlying pattern reads: prime motif (plus finishing motif) plus melodic motif plus concluding motif. The thematic unity of all the *Adagio* themes as well as their being modified patterns of the themes of the first movement, cannot be doubted.

Having completed this examination, we may now note the corner intervals. As seen in the following chart, they too remain the same as in the first movement.

First theme
    First group, C to B flat: The seventh.
    Second group, F to G: The ninth.
Second theme
    First group, C to C: The octave.
    Second group, F to G: The ninth.*
Third theme
    First group, E flat to D flat: The seventh.
    Second group, E to D sharp: The ninth.

5. BRIDGES AND CODA

Apart from the three themes, the substance of the *Adagio* contains only two small 'bridges' and a short coda. These two bridges both revolve round a specific element as their characteristic motivic feature, namely, the *finishing motif*.

The first bridge (bars 23–28) consists of a series of finishing motifs, and even its contour shows two finishing motifs and one concluding motif. The second bridge (bars 48–50) is formed exclusively by two long extended finishing motifs. The coda (bar 66 to the end), introduces the previously quoted chromatic 'particle', and includes the concluding motif in a dual shape. The second shape shows the motif in its familiar form (though transposed); but the first shape is a specific *Adagio* shape —that is, the *concluding motif is here formed through the melodic motif*, namely, a descending seventh:

* The ninth is obviously the 'inner' corner interval of this group, in which the F is felt as the lower corner. Yet the composer had to add an E flat as the concluding tonic. This would form the only deviation from the symmetry of corner intervals in the sonata.

Example 86

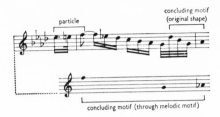

At the end of this movement a new feature appears:

Example 87

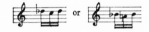

Small and inconspicuous as it looks, it is, doubtless, an intentional structural feature. For it indicates, as will be seen, one of the characteristic motivic elements of the following *Rondo*. Therefore, it will be dealt with in the next chapter.

6. ARCHITECTURAL KEYS

In concluding the analysis of the *Adagio*, it may be interesting to discover whether, as a parallel to the *Allegro*, some pivotal key relationships can also be discovered in this movement.

First, however, a still wider architectural problem will be touched upon. Only touched upon, because to probe into it thoroughly would be impossible within the frame of a single musical work: it is the problem of key relationships between the different movements of a composition.*
Suffice it to say that classical composers did endeavour to establish such a relationship; more specifically, they often expressed the basic motifs of their works through key relationships between the movements. In this sense the most 'plausible' key for the *Adagio* of the *Pathétique* would have appeared to be E flat, by which the relationship between the movements would have conformed to the prime cell. However, if the *Adagio* were in E flat the composer would be deprived of spelling the prime cell at its original pitch in the first bars of the *Adagio* and would thus somewhat destroy the symmetry of melody and mood.

Therefore, Beethoven chose the contrary motion of his prime cell as

* 'Thematic Key Relations', pp. 219–30, *The Thematic Process in Music*.

the element determining the key of the *Adagio*, and the second movement appears in A flat. And once contrary motion was decided upon as the basic idea, the further key-pattern of the movement developed in logical sequence. The following chart makes this clear:

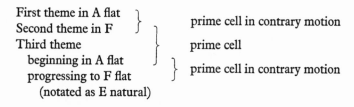

The remarkable phenomenon emerging from this chart is the comparative analogy to the first movement. For the pivotal keys of the *Allegro* are C, E flat, E natural, C, while the main keys of the *Adagio* are A flat, F natural, F flat, A flat. Or in other words the key pattern of the *Adagio* is the exact contrary motion of the key pattern of the *Allegro*.*

[* A musical example may make clearer this amazing interlocking of key-relationships, laid bare here by Réti.—ED.]

8

The *Rondo*

1. THE THEMATIC PATTERN ALSO ACTIVE IN THE *RONDO*

TURNING to the last movement, the *Rondo*, what strikes us first is that the motivic idea of its opening bars is *the prime motif in inversion*:

Example 88

We soon become aware, however, that it is not only the prime motif, but indeed the whole familiar thematic pattern, which is again audible in the *Rondo*. And though here again its character and combination are changed, its basic design—prime motif in C (plus finishing motif) plus prime motif in F plus concluding motif—clearly sounds from the *Rondo* theme:

Example 89

A word must be added about the one remaining element, the melodic motif. This motif from the *Adagio* seems to be absent in the *Rondo* theme. It was, it is true, a specific characteristic of the second movement. Yet it too, as will be seen, appears to be interwoven into all the themes

70

of the *Rondo*, in one way or another, though its important role was played in the *Adagio*, the 'melodic' movement.

2. ALL STRUCTURAL SHAPES MIRRORED IN THE *RONDO* THEME

The structural tie binding the *Rondo* theme to the preceding movements is not centred in the 'pattern' alone. Of course, the pattern as such makes the *Rondo* theme a derivative of the *Grave* and thus a part of the architecture of the whole work. But there are audible in the *Rondo* specific analogies to other thematic groups as well.

The prime motif of the opening, for instance, is interwoven with other elements which deserve attention. First, there are three opening notes forming an *auftakt*. They are easily recognizable as a literal (though transposed) repetition of the beginning of the second *Allegro* theme of the first movement:

Example 90

This could seem to be a casual similarity, not worthy of any attention in a structural sense, were it not for the fact that, in addition, another more inward connection between these two themes becomes visible. To uncover it, we may recall, as one of the characteristic features of the second *Allegro* theme, that 'varied version' of the prime motif, appearing there both in detail, through the mordent, and as an overall contour of the underlying harmonies:

Example 91

Now we see an imitation of this shape clearly emerging as one of the motivic elements of the first *Rondo* theme:

Example 92

Therefore, recognizing this twofold affinity, the one through the same *auftakt*, the second through the same phrase as a basic motivic element, there can hardly be any doubt that this affinity was formed by the composer quite intentionally.

However, another structural scheme, that of the *Adagio*, also makes its contribution. The second half of the *Rondo* theme, in its descending fifths, forms a clear replica of the second half of the first *Adagio* theme:

Example 93

Thus we see all the decisive sections of the preceding movements of the sonata combine, in order to build the opening theme of its last movement.

3. THE *RONDO* MOTIF

The *Rondo* has its own motif. It first emerged as that tiny phrase at the end of the *Adagio*:

Example 94

thus prophesying its appearance as an actual motif in the following movement. We may, therefore, call it the *Rondo* motif:

Indeed, it permeates the *Rondo* at all points. It is audible in the first bar, in the bass:

and it emerges as a particle in the soprano line, both in its original form and in inversion:

Above all, it also appears in the soprano line as a contour sounding from the melodic culmination of the theme:

4. PRIME CELL, SECOND GENERATION

To fully comprehend the specific design of the *Rondo* theme, one further feature—and this time one of the most decisive in the architecture of the whole work—has to be described. To this purpose we shall now include a few general observations in our analysis.

The prime cell, the basic shape of the sonata, has lived throughout the first two movements as a personality, so to speak, complete in itself. It has been changed from its original shape to its inversion, from its minor form to major, transposed to other pitches, and even clad in different versions. However, while the cell's appearance may have been altered, its inner individuality has remained constant—even while sounding in sequences:

Example 95

Even though groups and periods were formed in this way, no new and autonomous structural prime-cell phenomenon beyond its original idea, was created.

One of these cell-linkings deserves special attention. It is the combination of two consecutive prime cells:

Example 96

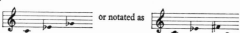

whereby one cell releases the next, so to speak, from its orbit. This pair of linked cells becomes a regular feature in the structural picture of the

Allegro. It is heard even in the sonata's opening bar, through the F sharp in the bass, added to the E flat in the soprano. It is also expressed through the relationship between the first and second *Allegro* themes—the first theme being in C, the second in E flat minor, thus spelling C, E flat, G flat—and through numerous other instances.

However, this shape is in one sense a kind of dead-end. For the whole harmonic idea of classical music tends toward a resolution of its shapes in a resolving cadence of dominant and tonic. And such a resolution is not even attempted within the shape C, E flat, G flat. This is shown through the dramatic outcry of the prime cell at the end of the recapitulation of the *Allegro*, when the prime cell C to E flat, with the F sharp as bass, finally flows into nothing—a rest (see Example 73).

Summing up, it may therefore be stated that the prime cell of the *Pathétique*, left to itself, or even linked to a second identical cell, represents an idea of the highest intensity, but one of unresolved tension.*

Only once in the course of these movements does a different phenomenon come to life. It is at the very end of the *Allegro*, when after that second outburst of the prime cell, another prime cell, this time in the major, is linked to the first in the minor. There the resulting shape was:

Example 97

and this shape is by no means an idea of unresolved tension, structurally or emotionally. For it bears the resolution through the resolving cadence, as seen above.

Of course, at the end of the movement this phenomenon could hardly acquire any architectural importance. In the last bar of a piece, in the form of a finishing cadence, no new structural element can be introduced.

But in the *Rondo* this idea is resumed and now it assumes a decisive role. Here this combination of the two prime cells, in minor and major (later to be varied to major and minor) forms the essence of the first *Rondo* theme. It becomes a motif, a kind of *second generation of the prime cell idea*, as derived from the union of the original elements.

---

* In general throughout this analysis, reference to the psychic or emotional sphere has been avoided. Whenever this emotional sphere is touched, it is for the purpose of making perceptible those correlating forces in which emotional or spiritual manifestations are brought about *through structural phenomena*.

We may call this new motif the *doubled prime cell*, and we see it rising in the first bars of the bass (a), then sounded twice in the second bar (b):

Example 98

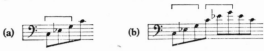

Above all, it floats through the dancelike figures of the soprano line as its melodic contour, culminating in the jubilantly thrice-repeated G, and thus leading the dramatic tension to its dénouement:

Example 99

5. ARCHITECTURAL RESOLUTION

The feature just described is one of the most decisive in the architecture of the sonata. Though its full significance in Beethoven's output cannot be comprehended in the analytical scheme of one work alone, it may at least be mentioned that the formal planning of all of Beethoven's works is centred on 'architectural resolution'.

In the *Pathétique* the cell which was heard throughout the whole sonata in forms such as:

Example 100

now suddenly appears in a new combination:

This minute alteration from

lends a quite specific appeal to the last movement. Indeed, this minute change forms the very core of the work's architecture.

However, to understand not only the spirit but also the structural consequences of this phenomenon, one must become aware of one further point. It is that through such a combination of two cells in minor and major a perfect fifth is formed.

We may recall that in the *Allegro*, fifths, and their inversions, fourths, were absent as structural features; then in the *Adagio* they became visible as melodic phrases; but only now, in the *Rondo*, do they rise to full motifs. For here the fifth, established through the formation of the doubled cell, is demonstrated as a structural derivative of the prime cell. It is therefore only logical that these perfect fifths and fourths assume a role of importance in the following part of the work. This will become apparent in the description of the second *Rondo* theme.

6. INTERESTING CORNER INTERVALS

Let us continue to examine the first *Rondo* section. Let us start from the corner interval of the theme—the ninth, G to A flat. The composer, after having concluded the theme, repeats the second half of it as an independent group:

Example 101

In this group no corner seventh or octave can be discovered. But, almost as if bent on proving the validity of his self-imposed rule through something like a text-book example, Beethoven lifts the line again in an annexed 'codetta' (see Example 102), first through the melodic motif to the seventh (C to B flat, which is the original pitch of the corner interval) and then immediately, in a rather striking alteration of the otherwise identical groups, to the octave. In other words, the composer repeats a group literally, merely differentiating the two occurrences by means of the corner intervals of the work, and thus clearly proves his consciousness of this particular feature:

Example 102

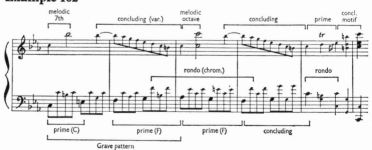

7. MOTIFS DETERMINE COUNTERPOINT

A small but significant feature may be pointed out here. It emerges in the first bar of the example above. There the collision between the B flat in the soprano part and the B natural in the bass represents a rather unusually discordant setting of voices for Beethoven's time. However, this setting appears most convincing on the basis of thematic structure, the soprano part being the melodic motif (corner interval) and the bass the *Rondo* motif. Thus we witness an example of motifs determining counterpoint.

8. A MOTIVIC CONTEST

The continuation of the bridging group in Example 102 (bars 18–33), reveals constant motivic combinations: prime motifs plus finishing or concluding motifs forming the substance, while perfect fourths and fifths also shine through. Moreover, the *Rondo* motif is often interpolated, sometimes in a chromatic version. And in one case a resumption of the doubled prime cell in contrary motion becomes audible.

Then comes a shaping which is quite important from an architectural point of view:

Example 103

Three decisive motifs occur here simultaneously. First, the prime cell in the glittering triplets of the soprano line and also in the shaping of the bass; second, the *Rondo* motif; and last but not least, as a crowning contour, the doubled prime cell (B flat, D, F), the melodic core of the first *Rondo* theme. Through the resumption of this first *Rondo* theme the whole section is framed into one structural unity.*

---

* This analysis is in general free from polemics. However, one example of the innumerable misleading comments on Beethoven's works may be quoted. This shows how dangerous it is to meddle with Beethoven's shapings without considering their structural meaning. In reference to the group above one widely used edition prints the following suggestion.

'The F³ was the highest key upon the pianoforte at the time this sonata was written, otherwise Beethoven would probably have carried the phrase up to

Let us compare this group with the next, a kind of sister group which repeats the same idea in a slightly different version. The difference between the two groups is that the first is centred on thirds only—that is, on the old prime motivic shapes—whereas the new group is formed by an interchange of these thirds with perfect fourths (emphasized by Beethoven through the *sforzato* on the A flat):

Example 104

This interchange between thirds, as the old motivic elements, and perfect fourths and fifths, as the new ones, becomes from here on a substantial feature in the thematic design of the movement. In fact, it increases to a rather exciting motivic play, a true contest between the old and the new motifs. And with this idea in mind, we will now examine the further course of the work.

9. FOURTHS AND FIFTHS FORMING A THEME

Thus we see that after having evolved fourths and fifths, through the foregoing, to definite motifs, the impulse of structural inevitability

---

A flat, whereby the passage would have gained greatly in brilliancy. This bar, therefore, might begin without hesitation upon A flat, as follows:'

Example 105

This editor was obviously not aware that it is the resumption of the main theme of this movement, namely:

Example 106

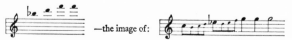

—the image of:

which he undertakes to 'correct', in order to add more 'brilliancy'.

induces the composer finally to *shape a theme from these elements*. In fact, the melodic content of the second *Rondo* theme consists in its opening group of plain fourths and fifths, embellished by a little phrase expressing the *Rondo* motif in its chromatic version:

Example 107

By introducing these intervals as the substance for his theme at this very point, Beethoven's consciousness of the whole phenomenon is too obvious to be denied. The full weight of the composer's intention, however, is only understood by realizing that this design represents the first instance in the *Pathétique* of the building of a melodic line—and, moreover, one forming the core of a theme—from shapes in which *no connection whatsoever with the prime cell or concluding motif can be discovered*.

This is a fact of tremendous importance in a structural sense. Here the old motifs do not shine out, and are not even interwoven into the design.

What has happened? Has the structural unity of the work suddenly been dissolved? We may remember that in the first *Rondo* theme the prime cells, though still appearing as the basic shapes, were developed into a new combination. We called this combination the 'doubled cell':

Example 108

From this shape the composer now takes an extract:

Example 109

and forms a new theme of it, the second *Rondo* theme. This shape is clearly a (contracted) replica of the first. And now we see why the motif of the doubled prime cell, this change from:

Example 110

79

THE THEMATIC PATTERN OF THE *PATHÉTIQUE*

must be considered as the core of the sonata's architecture. In introducing these fifths as autonomous thematic elements—that is, without pointing any longer to their origin from the doubled cells—a final architectural plan of the work takes shape. And this architectural plan is characterized by the contest between two contrasting ideas, namely *the shapes of tension* (as symbolized by the prime cell) and *the shapes of resolution* (as symbolized by the doubled cell and now by their substitutes, the fifths and fourths). It is indeed a contest rather than a replacement, for of course the old elements cannot disappear for ever. And naturally, the structural unity has not been broken, for the connection with the whole of the work is still preserved. This is accomplished through the old motivic characters, which accompany these fifths and fourths in the other voices:

Example 111

and still more emphatically through the last two bars of the theme, which clearly and definitely return to the basic shape of the *Pathétique* —prime cell plus finishing motif plus concluding motif, with even the melodic motif interwoven:

Example 112

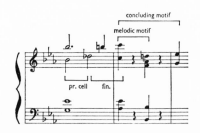

Moreover, since the preceding part of the theme expresses one long extended B flat,* it can easily be seen that the contour of the theme as a

[* Melodically speaking (see my Introduction).—ED.]

whole finally spells the old pattern once again. This indeed constitutes an architectural phenomenon of the first order:

Example 113

Incidentally, note the corner intervals of the theme: first group, B flat to B flat, the octave; second group, B flat to C, the ninth.

10. HARMONY AND MELODY AS COMPETITIVE THEMATIC FEATURES

The third *Rondo* theme then carries this principle of competition still further. For there the fourth and fifths form the *melodic* substance, while the old prime cell element is expressed through the constant *chording in thirds*:

Example 114

and to dispel all doubt that this was his idea, Beethoven, in the following repetition of the group, unfolds the line through syncopation so that the thirds are now to be heard *melodically* as well:

Example 115

However, there is still a higher degree of structural connection involved. For the *pattern* prime cell plus finishing motif plus concluding motif (with the melodic motif interwoven) sounds also from these fourths and fifths as a large melodic contour:

Example 116

Thus the logic of this amazing architecture is clear. The second generation, the fourths and fifths, have become the obvious elements of all the *Rondo* shapes. Yet the old basic pattern remains alive, and is still, it would seem, the prevalent idea.★

11. ARCHITECTURAL KEYS AGAIN

Another highly impressive architectural feature emerges from the fact that, at the very moment when the fourths and fifths emerge as the decisive elements in the sonata's structural design, the 'architectural keys'—these thematic pillars which in the preceding movements appeared in the form of thirds (that is in the old prime motivic shaping)—now suddenly emerge as fourths and fifths.

Section of the first theme, beginning	C	⎫ prime cell
Section of the first theme, end	E flat	⎬ fifth
Second theme, beginning	B flat†	⎬ fourth
Second theme, end	E flat	⎬ fourth
Third theme, beginning	A flat	⎬ fifth
Third theme, end	E flat	⎭

[★ Surprisingly, Réti makes no mention of the often-noticed relationship of this third *Rondo* theme to the first *Rondo* theme and thence to the second part of the first *Adagio* theme (see Example 93). Yet this relationship—the chain of falling fifths and rising fourths, in this case presenting a skeleton chain of Réti's 'concluding motifs'—is clearly an important element in the architectural 'plot' of the *Pathétique*.—ED.]

[† See my note on p. 80.—ED.]

However, here too, the old elements are not really dropped. For a prime motif (contrary motion) emerges, formed through *the beginnings of the three themes*:

First theme: C
Second theme: B flat
Third theme: A flat.

Thus, even with these great structural shapes, the old and new motifs are interwoven into one.

12. CONCLUSION

Since the whole *Rondo* is formed from the substance of the themes just described, there remains only the Coda to be dealt with. It is introduced significantly enough through the *Rondo* motif in *fortissimo* chords:

Example 117

Then, in the following group, which is the last in the sonata before its concluding bars, a shaping arises which leads that previously described struggle between the old and the new motifs to its highest intensification. This contest between the thirds and the fourths and fifths could hardly have been portrayed more intentionally, more obviously, than in the following jubilant shaping. Here the *Rondo* motif sounds simultaneously at the top as a contour:

Example 118

Then, in this contest, the prime cell, rising both in the soprano and in the lower voices, remains victorious, in a highly effective dissonant *fortissimo*:

83

Example 119

This discord (third bar of the example above) is indeed a genuinely Beethovenian manifestation. The composer could easily have sustained the preceding D flat major chord, a chord so fitting to the high F in the soprano part. However, at this decisive point, he wished to hammer out the prime cell idea with the greatest possible emphasis. Therefore, he led the left hand up to the E flat, forming a wonderful dominant ninth, not resolved until the following group—and thus almost recalling the dramatic dissolution toward the end of the first movement.

13. THE STORY OF THE *PATHÉTIQUE* IN TWO CHORDS

The resolving bars which follow echo the first *Rondo* theme:

Example 120

This little episode, however, is also quickly broken off, and is followed by a highlight of structural expression:

Example 121

For the whole story of the structural drama of the *Pathétique*, so to speak, is compressed in these two *pianissimo* chords. Both utter the prime cell, C to E flat. But the first chord joins to the cell an F sharp, thus recalling the idea of unresolved tensions from the first movements.

84

Then, when in the next bar the F sharp is changed to G, the resolution is achieved through the phenomenon of the *Rondo* itself, the doubled prime cell.

A concluding passage finishes the piece. In its realm of one bar and a half, it included all the basic features of the sonata: prime cell plus concluding motif, melodic motif, perfect fourth and fifth, even an indication of that contest between these intervals and the thirds, and finally the *Rondo* motif:

Example 122

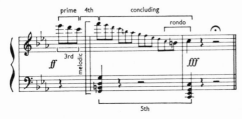

14. A TRIPLE *FORTE*

On the very last chord of the sonata, Beethoven placed a triple *forte*. This is a rather rare if not a unique marking in Beethoven's music. Apart from the *Kritische Gesamtausgabe*, which presents Beethoven's original, this *fff* is not found in the usual editions. The editors, obviously not knowing what to make of it, simply omitted it, probably considering it to be merely a great man's whim.

However, there is, as in all Beethoven's notation, a very real structural sense involved in this *fff*. The triple forte closes the structural cycle of the sonata.

The opening bar of the *Pathétique* was formulated in our analysis as a summation of the prime motif plus the finishing motif. Yet, the opening C minor chord with its *fp* stands as a separate unit somewhat outside the actual motif. Of course the prime cell is expressed through the whole arc beginning with the opening C to the E flat. But in the actual motivic phrasing, the first chord is an element in itself, after which the concrete motifs rise and fall:

Example 123

In this sense, and in the symmetry with the following bars, the first bar might be expected to have been preceded by an *auftakt*—perhaps the octave motif; but Beethoven dismissed this idea. He wanted the sound of the prime cell as the very start of the work. Thus, he gave up the idea of an opening *auftakt* and put, so to speak, a lone chord at the beginning, like a column at the entrance to a temple.

And the idea of this single, emphatic 'column-chord' remains alive throughout the whole sonata. A structural mind like Beethoven's could not do otherwise than finally, in some way, resolve this phenomenon.

Now the rest in the concluding bar of the sonata, after the last chord, is the traditional way of restoring the incomplete first bar of the specific movement, in this case the *Rondo*, to a full four-four measure. Through this the cycle of the third movement is completed. But by putting the *fff* on the last chord, a still wider cycle is closed. For, through this *fff*, the last chord is somewhat elevated, almost segregated, and converted into a response to the opening chord of the sonata. The pause on the following rest intensifies this meaning. The chord proceeds to the infinite whence it came.

9

The Musical Nature of the *Pathétique*

1. PHRASES BEHIND THE PHRASES

HERE, at the close of the analysis, let us review some of the general principles on which the technique of thematic structure is based. Although these principles have been seen at work throughout the whole analysis, their full meaning within the architectural design of the composition may only gradually become clear.

Let us recall those cases in which the working of a motif was described both in detail and as a wider contour, for here is centred one of the essentials of thematic structure. In fact, all the motivic elements of the *Pathétique*—prime cell, concluding motif and *Rondo* motif—appear invariably both as small, almost unnoticeable particles and as larger melodic shapes, or eventually even as huge architectural pillars.

However, the motifs not only appear in various degrees of size, but also in all thinkable forms of rhythm and accent; also different motifs or different forms of the same motif overlap or are interwoven in one another, or sometimes form shapes of which parts belong to different groups. Moreover, by transforming the different motifs of a work into higher units, or patterns, the themes and larger groups come into being.

Finally through a kind of *thematic resolution*—that is, through a specific alteration of the basic thematic idea—the design of the entire work is shaped as an expression of one unifying architectural plan.

In the conventional theoretical view all the structural connections from which a composition is formed are interpreted through *phrases and phrasing*. In this respect the smallest units are defined as *phrases*—although the theoreticians do not agree as to how long a phrase has to be; and starting from this premise, all groups and periods of a composition are explained as larger comprehensions of these phrases. By *phrasing*, on the other hand, is understood the characteristic shaping, and this is usually achieved by ligatures, through which the composer makes these phrases appear in their individual form.

This whole topic of phrasing has become one of the most problematic chapters in musical theory. For the discipline of phrasing seems to be founded on a tacit assumption that all musical utterances must be in compliance with an abstract schematic symmetry; and then this symmetry is thought to be based on certain imaginary accents which allegedly permeate every composition throughout its entire course. Many books have been written on this supposition, and lengthy comments have divided almost every classical work into hundreds of such phrases. One commentator argues with another about whether a few notes should, in applying a three-bar symmetry, be counted in one group, or, by applying a four-bar symmetry, included in the next; or whether a 'centre of gravity' of a phrase really coincides with the centre of rhythm, or should be regarded as postponed beyond the phrase; or whether in a certain group some 'strong beats have not had to be omitted' by the composer, and therefore in accordance with doctrine should be restored, and so on, and so on.

Yet little clarification of musical structure has resulted from such an endeavour. The reason for this is that compositions do not arise essentially from phrases, but from motifs. The phrases represent merely the characteristic outer shape which the motifs, these inner elements, assume from case to case. The motifs, however, constantly intermingle, their forces sometimes working parallel, sometimes in different or even contrasting directions.

Therefore, no definite scheme of phrasing can reasonably be applied to music, since every phrase, every series of notes in a living composition of higher structure, can be interpreted *from several angles simultaneously*. They can express one motif and at the same time form part of another. And it is ridiculous to discuss so circumstantially whether for instance the first note of the *Allegro* of the *Pathétique*, the C, forms the beginning of the *Allegro* or the end of the *Grave*. It is of course both at the same time.

Therefore, it should not be considered illogical to describe the notes from the beginning of the sonata in accordance with two interwoven or even contradictory aspects, as we did, for instance, in Example 10:

Example 124

Moreover, should the reader's own understanding of some detail call occasionally for a different motivic interpretation from the one given in our analysis, he may rest assured that both ideas can be right, if only each grew from, and tends toward, a logical thematic design. It is only natural that one might be sceptical of the idea that Beethoven, or any truly inspired composer, created his passages and figurations by coldly connecting motivic particles. But this is by no means the concept put forth in this analysis. What should be understood is merely that the creative mind of any genuine composer, at least the composer of the period under discussion, is so entirely and irresistibly filled by the structural elements from which he builds his work, that their force instinctively* and inevitably affects the content of the passages and figurations, even down to the most minute particle. This then excludes any non-motivic shape from the work.

Returning to the motifs and phrases in general, they may often be shaped to bring about a convincing symmetry, but no symmetry abstractly derived can ever be imposed upon the musical shapes.

Every composer knows that when it comes to the phrasing of his compositions, there is no definite rule governing it: there are always numerous possibilities from which to draw, and finally the composer must choose the strongest of them—those most appropriate to his thematic concept and to the nature of the specific instrument involved.

This should not be misunderstood, for the compositional picture of a work as formed through the phrases is by no means an unimportant factor. The phrased shape of a composition is synonymous with its appearance, its expression, and is no less important than appearance is to any phenomenon. The phrases constitute not only the surface but the very face of a work. However, as faces are often misleading and as there is still an inner life behind the outward appearance, there are in music *phrases behind the phrases,* and these are the motifs.

But in dwelling upon the dissection which is inevitably involved in every structural examination, one is inclined to lose sight of the higher synthesis. That is, one is inclined to forget that motifs are not merely structural bricks but are a part of the flow, the song which is composition.

To demonstrate this most essential nature of the thematic phenomena, let us follow the compositional flow of the *Pathétique* through for the last time.

2. FOLLOW THE MOTIVIC TUNE

Let us recall the beginning of the *Pathétique*. The phrase in the first bar (called in this analysis the prime motif) is sounded and repeated at a

* Cf. 'Is the Thematic Process Conscious or Subconscious?' p. 233–47, *The Thematic Process in Music.*

higher pitch. Then these two bars are themselves repeated an octave higher, and a cadencing ornament (called the concluding motif) is added. All this is familiar to us. But now we may ask: What is the innermost compositional process here involved?

The composer certainly did not follow any theoretical scheme or mathematical rule. He did not figure out how certain phrased particles could be fitted together. But he did, so to speak, improvise. He followed a little motif which sprang up in his mind—he transposed, reiterated, varied it, just as a gypsy, for instance, would improvise a little tune on his fiddle. It is a purely *musical* procedure. Yet, trying to describe its result, we can only explain it as thematic structure.

The further course of the *Grave* reveals exactly the same musical endeavour. The composer–improvisor simply continues to utter his motivic tune again and again (bars 5–9). Naturally, however, he cannot proceed indefinitely in this way, it would finally produce unbearable monotony. Thus, he remembers the other, the second little phrase with which he had closed his opening section:

Example 125

and he interpolates it now in his improvisational line, sounding it twice, and dwelling fiddler-like on one tone:

Then he returns to the first 'tune' again—which still sounds in his ear in this version:

or in abbreviation:

but now it glides from his mind as:

What is the meaning of this? Is it a new figure? In the analysis we would call it an inversion. However, in the composer's mind it sprang up again as a purely instinctive alteration, a slight 'variation' of the original phrase. To this again the second phrase is added, as a chromatic passage, but now the newly discovered figure, the inversion, is worked in twice:

Example 126

Thus the *Grave* has come into existence.

In the example below the whole *Grave* can be seen as an improvisational intoning of two motifs. (The motifs are notated without any rhythmical distinction, somewhat in accordance with the indefinite character of an improvisation; also, notes which form both the end of a motif and the beginning of a new one are notated twice.)

Example 127

3. TEMPO OF THE *GRAVE* SOUNDING FROM THE *ALLEGRO*

After the close of the *Grave*, the now established thematic tune (or note-series) revolves in continuing improvisation in the composer's mind. However, it is no longer merely a repetition of the original little phrases, but a combination of these motivic shapes *in a certain succession*. This is the melodic skeleton which still sounds in the composer's ear:

Example 128

(a)

In making it fluent and stretching it rhythmically, he changes the E flat to E natural and—the idea of the *Allegro* theme has emerged:

(b)

By repeating this shape an octave higher, just as in the case of the *Grave*, and by adding a cadencing conclusion, the whole *Allegro* theme arises.

But it is not only the verbal line of the theme which is revealing. For, as we know, when the original motif of the *Grave* is repeated many times, one little shape of it, the cell C to E flat, finally remains sounding in the ear. Now the decisive phenomenon is that this cell continues to sound from the *Allegro* theme even in the same tempo as in the *Grave*:

Example 129

To be sure, it does not sound in the *actual* tempo, which of course in the *Allegro* is eight times as quick, but *in the tempo of the shape C to E flat*, which sounds through the line as its inner music. Shaped through these inner accents the *Allegro* theme appears like this (bars 11–19):

Example 130

which clearly represents the continuance of the motivic intonation of the *Grave*.

And this intonation continues beyond the theme. For, after the repetition which ends in a half close, the composer reiterates the 'inversion' from the *Grave* at transposed pitch:

Example 131

(inversion) prime motif plus fin. motif   now transposed

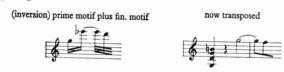

and closes through the cadencing ornament, which is the concluding motif, to the tonic (bars 33–35):

Example 132

Then the first motif is again sounded twice (first in inversion, then as the original prime motif plus finishing motif). It sounds in the *Grave* tempo (as seen in the following contour), but now adapted to the *Allegro* by the interwoven figurations (bars 35–43—cf. Ex. 38):

Example 133

So we see again and again the continuous flow of the two *Grave* motifs forming the essence of the *Allegro*. Thus, in this essence, in this skeleton, a multitude of figurations and combinations derived from one motivic substance is let loose to produce the final, definite shape of the *Allegro*. And this moulding of numerous combinations into a higher unity is what distinguishes a work of art from a pure improvisation. Yet the innermost principle is the same. Thematic structure is improvisation passed through technique.

Let us return for a moment to the development section of the *Allegro*, and trace its inner contour—its 'thematic song'. The reader is urged to check the following outline against the score; only through such a comparison does it make sense. No note has been changed. At one point a D, omitted by Beethoven for grammatical reasons, has been restored— restored, not invented, for Beethoven's D is clearly heard a little later in the analogous bar (marked by an asterisk):

Example 134

Continued overleaf.

4. A THEMATIC SONG

The whole shape of the *Pathétique* should be comprehended as a musical improvisation, a true thematic song around a few motifs. Heard in this way, thematic structure does not complicate the understanding of a composition; rather is it the only way of making the shape of a composition fully transparent and comprehensible.

In the *Pathétique*, the composer, consciously and subconsciously, has moulded a unified body of sound from a few small motifs; these motifs unite to form a thematic pattern; and this pattern, the pattern of the *Grave*, permeates the entire work. It becomes the skeleton of all themes in all movements; it determines the modulations, the figurations and the bridges, and above all, it provides an outline for the overall architecture of this great sonata.

Section 2

Thematic Structure and Form

The Sonata *Appassionata*

1. SOME CLARIFICATIONS

AT the beginning of our investigations, the term *cell* was introduced. The cell proved a useful concept through which a multitude of motivic variants could be readily demonstrated. Now, however, with a deeper insight into motivic connections, the nature of these cells may be described more precisely.

It would be misleading, as stated earlier, to conceive the cell as a (so to speak) mystical phenomenon from which the composer built his work. The cell is indeed one of the variants of a motif. Or, more specifically, it is the variant which represents the shortest extract of a motif, its contour.

In the *Pathétique*, there are three main forms of the prime motif; we called the first the cell, the second the motif, and the third the motif in chromatic form. However, this should not create the idea that the variant which we call the cell would have to be considered the musical fountain from which the composer's phantasy sprang. We may on the contrary assume as almost a certainty that the motif, as seen in the opening bar, was the first spark to emerge in the composer's mind. However, once he had chosen a certain shape as his main motif, then in the process of revolving, which is after all composing, it was only natural that that variant which formed the most concise extract, and which we therefore call the cell, plays a more and more significant role in the building of the work—though in some compositions, as stated earlier, the extract may never be heard in its literal form.

2. THE PRIME CELLS OF THE *APPASSIONATA*

Having thus clarified the principle as such, the function of prime cells in the *Appassionata* may be attributed to three different shapes. The term prime cell, however, will henceforth be used only in reference to one of these shapes:

Example 135

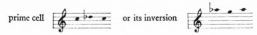

The second cell shape will be called:

The third shape will be referred to as:

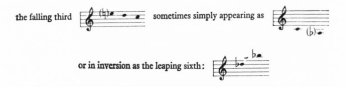

3. MOTIVIC INTERVALS

In an analysis one is forced to enumerate a multitude of details which in the musician's mind are understood as a unity; and some readers, who view the outward picture rather than the inner principle, may be inclined to argue as follows. Since almost all existing intervals appear gradually as motivic features in the analysis of a work, and as every motif appears both in inversion and in all kinds of variants, cannot then practically every thinkable shape be identified with one of the motivic elements? Does it not seem as if the list of motifs from one piece could easily be applied to any other piece, and the equation still remain balanced?

But one need only try to apply the elements of the *Pathétique*, for instance, to the *Appassionata*, to realize how false such a supposition is. Indeed, objections of this type would not even be worthy of mention were it not that, by refuting them, some principles of thematic structure can be made clearer.

Naturally, in any large-scale piece almost all of the few existing intervals are heard, and even in a more or less motivic role. Yet the individual form of a composition is not built by the use of so many and such-and-such intervals as bricks, but by the specific and always different way in which these elements are introduced, developed and finally combined into higher units.

Theoretically, in the *Appassionata*, for instance, no less than six intervals emerge from our prime motivic list: the second, third, fourth, fifth, and sixth. With a view to the living structure of the composition, however, the picture appears quite differently, because each of these intervals is seen specifically shaped, with its characteristic accent and rhythm, and often even bound to a certain pitch—in brief, each bears a definite musical meaning.

Therefore, besides the fact that a composition is built up by certain combinations and groups of motifs (the patterns), rather than through motivic particles or intervals, one must realize that even these intervals assume specific individualities. Thus in the *Appassionata* the fifth is primarily a *falling* fifth, the fourth an *ascending* interval. Analogously, the basic appearance of the third is a *stepwise descent*, while the sixth *leaps* upwards. But should a third occasionally appear in an ascending form, it does so only as a clear contrary motion to a descending third immediately preceding it—for instance in the opening bar of the sonata. Through much of the work this 'rule' is observed fairly strictly. Naturally, as the work proceeds, these features become somewhat transformed; nevertheless, the original concept remains even then too clear to be doubted.

4. VARIANTS AND PARTICLES

Certain principles, as described above, govern the whole sphere of motivic variants—or in other words, the structural role and meaning of any motivic feature depends always on the way in which it is introduced and developed. In the *Pathétique* the first shape spelling the cell in the minor:

Example 136

is given out within the first four bars alone half a dozen times. When then in the fifth bar this same shape emerges in the major:

it will doubtlessly be understood as a variant of the first. And the chromatic version appearing in bar 7 will also be understood as a variant.

And if the cell in the major is sounded several times in an emphatic way, then the ear will even grasp the sixth as its inversion:

(c) [music] or (d) [music]

The *Appassionata* contains some fascinating examples of this. First, besides the original prime cell formed through a minor second:

Example 137

(a) [music]

there is a variant of the prime cell in the major:

(b) [music]

Moreover, if the prime cell is expressed in bar 27–28 as follows:

(c) [music]

whereas the next bar reads:

(d) [music]

then hardly anyone would fail to understand the second type as a variant of the first, so that in this way another variant of the prime cell emerges, reading:

(e) [music]

Or if in bar 10 the cell appears in this shaping:

(f)

then we would certainly not hesitate to accept the shapes appearing two and three bars later, namely:

(g) 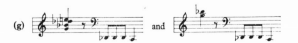 and

as derivatives of the first. Moreover, we would finally recognize the smaller phrase in itself as a part of the prime cell:

(h)

even if no longer within the wider shape. From now on we shall call this half of the prime cell the *particle*, and we recognize it, for instance, in:

bars 15–16   bars 26–27   bar 55

(j)   or   *sfp*   or

One of the figures demonstrated above (see *g*):

(k)

assumes gradually some significance as a motivic feature of its own. In fact, it emerges as a kind of inversion already in the bass of the opening bars of the sonata, as follows:

(m)

Its most characteristic appearance, however, is in the later 'principal theme', where in bar 36 it is to be seen in the following shaping:

(n)

forming a descending fourth, broken by an A flat, whereas in the case demonstrated above (*g*), it formed a third, broken by a D flat. For the sake of identification we shall call this motif the broken third or broken fourth.

As a last element we list a motif of note-repetition, just as in the *Pathétique*. It has come into being as a 'particle' of a particle, so to say. This motif appears in the *Appassionata* often in a special rhythm of three eighth notes followed by a sustained note:

(P)

recalling the famous rhythm of the Fifth Symphony.

5. ARPEGGIO MOTIF AND *APPASSIONATA* RHYTHM

Two specific elements have to be added to the motivic shapes already described. First the form of broken triads, such as:

Example 138

(a)

or broken chords of the seventh:

(b)

This use of broken chords will prove to be one of the motivic characteristics throughout the whole sonata: we will call it the arpeggio motif. Finally we may again point to a rhythmical feature. It is the rhythm in which the sonata opens:

(c)

This type of rhythm, too, assumes motivic character and we will refer to it as the *Appassionata* rhythm.

6. LIST OF MOTIFS

Example 139

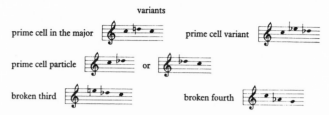

To this list must be added the two particular features:

Arpeggio motif: referring to the characteristic of broken chords

Appassionata rhythm: referring to the rhythm of the beginning.

The first movement of the sonata will henceforth be referred to as the *Allegro*, the second as the *Andante*, the third as the *Finale*, while the coda of the *Finale* will be referred to as the *Presto*.

7. THE THEMATIC PATTERN

Though the preceding tabulation, as with the *Pathétique*, may have appeared somewhat circumstantial, the structure of the work will now unfold all the more readily.

This is the opening group of the sonata:

Example 140

Here we see the *pattern* from which all the themes of the work are formed. The pattern evolves logically as a summation of the three prime elements: (1) prime cell; (2) fifth and fourth; and (3) the falling third. In this first theme, the part as far as the end of bar 2 expresses the fifth and fourth, while bar 3 spells the prime cell (in the major), to which the falling third is added as a little annexe in conclusion.

In addition, however, this whole group sounds as an expression of the pitch C. And since the ensuing group, as seen in Example 141, repeats the first one a semitone higher, and is followed by another group expressing the C again, the whole of the opening period represents a

Example 141

huge prime cell in itself (C, D flat, C). To demonstrate this and other
features, two or more lines may henceforth be applied almost regularly,
the upper line showing Beethoven's text, the lower giving the contour;
in this way the structural idea will be made clear. Therefore it is particularly the contour formed by a transparent chain of motifs, which in the
present example attracts our attention (see Example 141).

A kind of repetition of the group just described follows, whereafter
a new thematic section arises (bar 24):

Example 142

Here that great process of combining and revolving—the essence of
Beethoven's structural shaping—starts again. In trying to unravel this
melodic line, we discover that its substance is again the prime cell,
B flat, C flat, B flat, on which a fourth* is so to say, put astride:

* This fourth appears here as a kind of variant of the original pitch. The
original pitch of this motif, as heard in the opening bars, is C to F, while it now
appears as C flat to F flat. This motivic pitch, alternating from F minor

to F flat major

permeates the whole movement.

Example 143

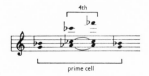

Moreover, the F flat in this shape, linked to the two E flats (the one preceding, the other following), forms a second prime cell, E flat, F flat, E flat:

Example 144

Thus we see the pattern emerging in this theme too. It grows here, as demonstrated in the above example, from a combination of two prime cells interwoven in such a way that the other cell element, the fourth, is heard at the same time.

Yet one of the basic elements seems to be absent: the falling third. However, it too follows immediately (in chromatic form) as the conclusion of the period:

Example 145

During all this, the left hand proceeds mostly on one tone, thus hardly, as it seems, producing any motivic shaping at all. Yet connecting these slight flickering chords of an inconspicuous 'accompaniment' to the coherent whole, a startling counterpoint emerges, reflecting literally the line of the right hand. The contour of the bass of Example 142 reads:

Example 146

Such motivic imitation is continued in the remaining part of the group, where the left hand features two falling thirds, through which the analogy to the corresponding shape in the right hand becomes complete:

Example 147

8. THE 'PRINCIPAL THEME'

The ensuing section is often referred to as the 'principal theme', owing no doubt to its melodic intensity and meticulous symmetry. Otherwise no structural reason can be found for elevating just this group above all others. Later we will discuss this subject more thoroughly.

The melodic arc in which this theme rises contains such an abundance of motivic combinations that one is at a loss to know where to begin. A series of motivic lines may again prove the clearest way:

Example 148

First, contour I shows that in this theme, too, the melodic kernel, though almost hidden beneath a contrasting surface, is indeed the prime cell in inversion, sounding twice through the accents of this beautiful shape. In contour II the second cell-element, the falling third, appears in a similarly symmetric form. Yet contour III is, in a higher architectural sense, perhaps the most interesting of all. For here we see that this theme too, though in a different key, remains embedded in the chief elements, prime cell and fourth at their original pitch—a phenomenon of a most impressive nature. Let us review the facts once again. The prime elements of the sonata at their original pitch, familiar to us from the beginning, read:

Example 149

Now a new theme in A flat major arises. This new theme is formed by the old motivic substance, which has of necessity, however, been transposed to the new key, as seen in Example 148. Yet the composer manages to have the old elements sound at their original pitch as well, even though the new theme itself is in a different key. (See contour III of the Example 148.)

Then the concluding part of this section reads as follows:

Example 150

Note especially the motivic nature of the ornaments, spelling the prime cell idea. Here the prime cell is intensified to the utmost.

9. A SCHEME OF CHARACTERISTIC CHORDS

In the next group—which, by the way, is the fourth in the exposition —what attracts our attention particularly is the striking similarity to the preceding theme:

Example 151

A still more convincing analogy becomes visible in the following comparative chart. Here the four themes are symbolized through four characteristic chords:

Example 152

As to the detail of the fourth theme, all the basic elements again appear: the falling third followed by the fourth forms the soprano line, while in the bass the whole period is embedded in the prime cell (A flat, B double flat, A flat). Thus the pattern is once again complete:

Example 153

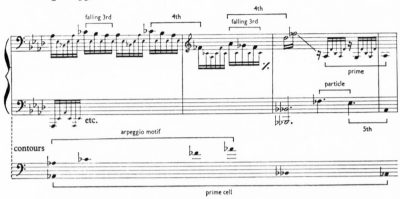

One more feature of interest is included in this theme. It is the arpeggio motif, which in the preceding sections appeared merely as a kind of motivic figuration. Here it emerges as the backbone of the structural shaping,* a variant at original pitch—A flat, C (flat), F (flat). Cf. Example 152, first and second lines.

This section is followed by a fifth section, which, however, does not represent a group of its own, but merely forms an annexe to the former group, and shows all the characteristics of a concluding coda or codetta. In the shaping of this last section, both the prime cells themselves and the motif known as the particle (that is, half of the prime cell) are the predominant features. The concluding bars, each bar an octave lower than the former (Example 154(b)) repeat the old combination: fourth plus particle at the pitch heard in the second thematic section (Example 154(a)).

Example 154

(a) Second section

---

* It must be considered a remarkable phenomenon that an element of such an indefinite nature as this arpeggio motif, consisting not of a certain phrase but of a manner of chording, could turn out to be an intentional structural idea from which the inner shape of themes is formed. It shows that in Beethoven's music hardly any element can be discovered, no matter how inconspicuous and casual it may at first appear, which may not later be elevated to a real structural feature. Were it not for this quality as a theme-building force, it would hardly have been worthwhile to register these figurations as motifs at all.

(b) Last section

Also the right hand of this passage (bars 62–65) elaborates inverted prime cells in its figuration. By reducing the octaves to unisons, we recognize the motif of note-repetition, as heard in the opening group of the sonata.

10. ARCHITECTURAL MOTIFS

The development and recapitulation are naturally built from the same elements as the exposition, so that their dissection may be left to the reader: only a few characteristic features may be touched upon. First there is key relationship. The key from which the development arises is E natural. Thus the prime cell (inversion) speaks from the architectural corners of the first movement:

Example 155

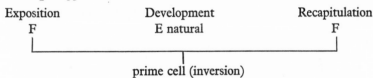

The modulations in bars 79–91, too, are carried out in the spirit of the prime cell.

In the coda, the prime cell is constantly thrown out in a most emphatic accentuation, in order to finally resolve into the fifth:

Example 156

Continued overleaf.

Now, through the long sustained C at the end, the whole movement would seem to sound as an expression of C.⋆ And since the second movement represents D flat, and in the *Finale* we fall again to C,⋆ the sonata itself appears as a prime cell of gigantic shape.

However, this is not the whole of the architectural phenomenon involved. For though C is the soprano contour of the first movement, its actual key remains F. Through this the key relationship between the *Allegro* and the *Andante* is F to D flat—that is, the falling third. Thus, one architectural motif formed through the contour, another through the keys, emerges in the *Appassionata*. Moreover, the relationship between these two shapes spells the third cell-element, the falling fifth. The motivic quality of this amazing design becomes visible in the following chart:

Example 157

[⋆ Réti refers to the soprano line, and means, as so often, 'melodically speaking' (see my Introduction).—ED.]

II

Sonata *Appassionata,*
Andante and *Finale*

1. TRANSPARENT SYMMETRY

THE second movement (*Andante con moto*) is a theme with variations. Even a first glance reveals that the old pattern—prime cell plus fifth plus falling third—forms the structural substance of this movement too. Moreover, the pattern is shown in a highly impressive new shaping. For while in the first movement the cell motifs appear either side by side, or in interwoven combinations, it is evidently the linking of these same motifs into one contrapuntal unity which constitutes the structural idea of the *Andante.*

Example 158

For instance:

The detailed scheme of the first period of the theme follows:

Example 159

113

However, to comprehend fully the amazing logic of this design, the motivic plan of the shapes of the right hand alone (soprano and tenor) may be pointed out specifically:

Soprano: Prime cell—note repetition—note repetition—prime cell.

Tenor: Note repetition—prime cell—prime cell—falling third.

The second part of the theme completes this scheme of unmatched symmetry:

Example 160

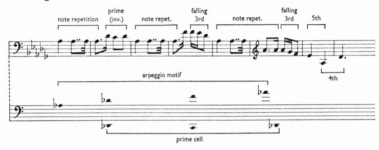

Here the falling thirds come to the foreground. The striking feature, however, is again the contour, which discloses the arpeggio motif as the backbone of this thematic shape also.

The variations, as almost literal repetitions of the theme, require no detailed analysis. Worthy of special attention, however, is the fact that the gradual resolving of the melody into open chords, a technique which in other classical works may be regarded as a mere routine in the structure of variations, here assumes a specific meaning. For it represents the idea of an evolving arpeggio motif, and in this way embraces the whole movement.

Interestingly enough, these arpeggio triads appear occasionally altered to figurations of the prime cell:

Example 161

Incidentally, through the series of variations, a constant key-relationship, primitive yet significant, emerges between the parts of the *Andante*, as follows: D flat, A flat, D flat, A flat, D flat, etc.—or in other words, a series of fifths.*

[* Again, melodically speaking.—ED.]

2. THIRTEEN CHORDS

The last variation reiterates the theme with only slight variances. The conclusion of the original theme was:

Example 162

(a)

but now it reads:

(b)

What has happened?

The original line, moving to an interrupted cadence, has reached its goal, D flat, in a *pianissimo* chord of the diminished seventh. The *fermata* on it symbolizes a moment of contemplation at the end of a dreamlike *Andante*. However, as in a dream, the call of life may have slumbered, but certainly did not cease to exist. Or to say this in musical terms, the greater architectural idea of the sonata was still alive behind the *Andante*, waiting for its fulfilment. D flat, with its inherent strength as a part of the prime cell, is the point of awakening. The chord of utter *pianissimo* is repeated *fortissimo*—and repeated again thirteen times in the stimulating rhythm of the beginning of the *Finale*:

Example 163

This thirteen times repeated diminished seventh, from a purely formalistic aspect, would appear a hollow procedure—no student should try to imitate this. Here, however, in their wider architectural connection, these accentuated D flats rise to an all-impressive utterance. By reinforcing the D flat idea which the whole of the *Andante* represents, and by linking it to the C of the preceding *Allegro* and the C of the following *Finale*, these chords create a giant prime cell, sounding over the whole sonata, comparable to a huge arc encircling a great building.

From here the line whirls down in a long passage, of which the motivic detail and its contour, the arpeggio motif, are easily recognized:

Example 164

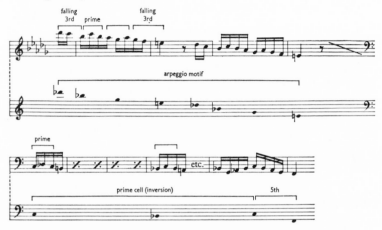

As can be seen, the passage concludes in a kind of prime-cell trill, finally descending through the fifth to the tonic. Here the main body of the *Finale* starts.

3. A CYCLE OF PERIODS

There is a little phrase which, in constant figurations, permeates the whole *Finale*. It is worthwhile taking a glance at its motivic detail:

Example 165

Within its small space this figure contains no less than the prime cell, the fourth (both at original pitch), the falling third, and the arpeggio motif. Then, through a repetition of this phrase a semitone higher, a first period of the *Finale* is initiated, which as a whole expresses the prime cell; this is somewhat analogous to the beginning of the sonata.

Perhaps the true thematic melody of this period, however, sounds from its bass line, reading:

Example 166

A clearer expression of the pattern than that of this thematic line—consisting, so to say, of nothing *besides* the pattern—is hardly thinkable.

This first period of the *Finale* is followed by another in which the soprano figurations of the first are repeated literally; to this, however, a partly altered bass-line is linked to a more melodically outspoken 'theme':

Example 167

Let us examine this line. It is the prime cell, the old prime cell at original pitch (C, D flat, C), which cries from the melodic contour of this theme.

However, this second period is followed by a third, carrying a new thematic bass—and the melodic contour of this bass is again the prime cell, but now no longer the prime cell in the version of, and at the pitch of, the first movement, but at the pitch and in the form of the second movement:

Example 168

From a structural aspect this certainly constitutes an exciting fact: The thematic shapes of the *Finale* are built in clear succession from the main shapes of the first and second movements of the sonata.*

4. WHICH IS THE THEME?

Our attention may now be directed to an observation which will be discussed more specifically later. We mean the appearance of an unusual number of different thematic groups within the beginning of the *Finale*. All these groups are different in melodic shape, though one evolves from the other; all, in a sense, are equal in importance, though obviously arising in one uninterrupted cycle of increasing melodic and emotional intensity.

Which of these groups should be called the theme? Or should one perhaps be regarded as the first theme and another as the second? At present this may be left as a question only; an answer will be attempted later.

5. DOUBLE COUNTERPOINT

Another interesting feature, though of more local importance, emerges from the fact that group III (bars 36–50) is written as an impressive example of double counterpoint.† Therefore it is only natural that the following group (IV—bars 50–64) appears as an inversion of the foregoing.

This effect of double counterpoint is subsequently applied to a

[* It might be pointed out that the 'contour' of Example 168 also presents Réti's 'prime cell variant' (Example 137e) from the first movement; and this strengthens his later argument concerning the 'architectural resolution' in the *Presto*. The example here is mine.—ED.]

† Counterpoint, as a compositional technique, is in its strict sense applied only to that style of polyphony from which it developed historically. In the following period, the period of Haydn, Beethoven and Brahms, where the compositional line is formed through series of compact chords and figurative combinations rather than through voices, the concept of counterpoint can be applied merely in a somewhat transcribed sense. In spite of this, or perhaps all the more for this reason, an example of such double counterpoint in this more complicated style has to be acknowledged as a compositional achievement of particular charm and originality. And incidentally, the slight differences in the figurations between the two groups are not necessitated, as one might perhaps think, by an insufficiency of contrapuntal quality, but by the fact that Beethoven even here invariably delights in including variants of the motivic phrasing.

number of shapes in the *Finale*. One might say that the structural idea of the first movement of the *Appassionata* is to spell the motifs, the idea of the second movement to spell them in counterpoint, and of the *Finale* in double counterpoint. But, apart from the inaccuracy of such a statement, it would not pierce to the core of the musical structure as a phenomenon. For counterpoint as such, even counterpoint of motifs, though often an important structural effect, never builds musical architecture, nor does it lead to its resolution. This resolution is brought about through the motivic forces themselves.

It is hardly necessary to analyse the remainder of the *Finale* in every detail; its substance is clear enough. The old elements of the pattern, in ever new combinations, form the structural essence—as for instance in the ensuing group (bars 64–76), which represents the fifth in the exposition. Then, in the following groups, an example of double counterpoint is heard again, although here, behind figurations, it is less obvious (bars 76–96).

Before the exposition draws to its conclusion, another prime-cell shape, caught within a rising and a descending scale, deserves mention (bars 104–105):

Example 169

6. ARCHITECTURAL KEYS OF THE *FINALE*

The development is reached through the shape of the 'particle', formed through a step from a diminished seventh on a G flat down to the tonic F:

Example 170

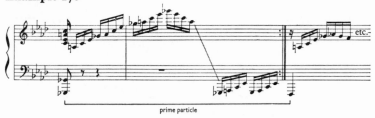

prime particle

However, since figurations of the diminished seventh continue over the F, as seen in the example above, the tonic is transformed into a dominant minor ninth of B flat.

7. 'NEW THEME' IN THE DEVELOPMENT

As often happens in Beethoven's music, the development produces a kind of new theme. The introduction of a new thought in a development has long been regarded as a rather revolutionary and even problematic act, of which the structural logic could be questioned. Such doubts, however, would never have been raised, had musicians been trained from the beginning to comprehend compositional shapes from a thematic point of view.

The 'new theme', for instance, presents so obviously the old prime-cell shape that it cannot in any way disturb the structural unity of the work:

Example 171

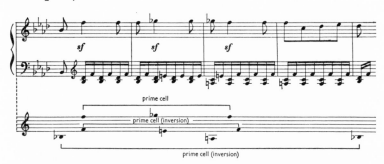

The rhythmic overlapping of the otherwise parallel motifs of the right and left hands is worthy of note. The group is then repeated, followed by a period representing a kind of motivic inversion of the first (see Example 172).

[* The reader will no doubt notice for himself a point which Réti omits to mention—the overlapping inverted 'prime cells' as a counterpoint to the main finale idea, in bars 134–37. The example here is mine.—ED.]

Example 172

8. RESOLUTION

As the recapitulation nears its climax, the 'prime-cell scales' referred to earlier rise and fall again. This time the scales are in the soprano part and the chords are in the bass; thus we have double counterpoint again:

Example 173

The scales rise and fall twice. Then tempo and dynamics increase, and the scales are interrupted by two exciting bars, in which this cell-version, F natural, G, F natural, is changed to its original motivic shape, G, F sharp, G:

Example 174

from which a last scale falls to the tonic F.

The famous *Presto* march follows. No one who knows the *Appassionata* doubts that here the musical and emotional climax of the sonata has been reached. Therefore, the answer to the question 'By what architectural means is this climax accomplished?' constitutes one of the focal points in the analysis of the work.

The decisive shape, thrown out most emphatically, reads as follows:

Example 175

Is this not the old variant of the prime cell? The one which in the first movement emerged in this form:

introduced as a sequel to:

Its essence as a derivative of the original cell cannot be doubted.* Now, in the *Presto*, it appears with a slight variance. The shape from the *Allegro*, transposed to the present pitch, would read:

whereas now it reads:

But this present variant is harmonically an expression of the combination of tonic plus dominant. Or, in other words, what we see happening here is again the phenomenon of architectural resolution. We witnessed it in the *Pathétique*, although there it was realized by means of a different technique. In both sonatas, however, the tension is led in this way to tonal fulfilment.

In the *Pathétique* the core of the architecture was centred in the progression from

[* If this seems far-fetched, it is perhaps because Réti overlooked the presence of the 'prime-cell variant'—and in its new form as an 'architectural resolution' —earlier in the *Finale*. See my note on p. 118.—ED.]

through which the resolving mood of the *Finale,* with its fifths and fourths, was brought about.

Now, in the *Appassionata,* the original prime cell

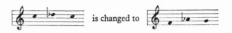

and this second shape is seemingly differentiated from the original form through only a minute alteration, yet the two shapes in their structural and emotional aspects are worlds apart. And it is a particular structural subtlety that this decisive variant, which accomplishes the resolution, is formed through shaping the prime cell as a third, that is through linking the cell to another of the prime elements of the work. In this case it had to be a rising instead of a falling third.

It is, therefore, only natural that this decisive shape forms the core of the *Presto* theme. In fact the whole period, in its essence, is none other than an uninterrupted utterance of this one resolving shape:

Example 176

Through adding the figurations of the arpeggio motif to this contour, Beethoven's text, as seen above, comes to life.

The other basic elements, the fifths and fourths, are also included through both the ending and re-beginning (*auftakt*) of the group:

Example 177

After this group, in the minor, which concludes in a half close, the next group (Example 178), repeating the same idea, still more triumphantly in the major (A flat), leads back to the tonic:

Example 178

Then the old figurations are resumed. The peak is reached when the resolving shape is again sounded, now displayed as open chords:

Example 179

Moreover, the other prime element, the fourth, is now sounded simultaneously as a counterpoint in the bass, with trumpet-like emphasis:

Example 180

In the ensuing conclusion, an effect of the utmost architectural intensity is included. It is the fact that now, when that resolving variant the tonic-dominant variant of the prime cell has been reached, the old (we might almost call it the 'atonal') cell vanishes suddenly from the picture. These concluding bars are the only group of the sonata which is free of any indication of the old prime cell, C, D flat, C. C itself is still heard a few times, as a corner accent from the top, as a recollection. Then it, too, falls in long arpeggios through the fifth to the real tonic F. And the symbol of finality, the F, not the C, remains the last note.

9. ARCHITECTURE THROUGH RHYTHM

Recalling the whole course of the sonata, we become aware of the fact that another idea of resolution, analogous to that just described in the melodic–harmonic structure, comes into being through its rhythmical design.

The rhythmical characteristic of the first movement was the so-called *Appassionata* rhythm (Example 138(c)). This rhythm, full of tension and excitement, though often a somewhat subdued excitement, spreads in more or less varied shapes through the whole *Allegro*. But even from the gentle solemnity of the *Andante* it is audible, for instance:

Example 181

or still more distinctly from the double-dotted quavers of the second part of the theme:

And the rhythm sounds no less in the *Finale* from the flickering sixteenths of the bass:

or even from the main thematic lines themselves:

But with the resolving *Presto* this rhythm disappears completely, and is replaced by the straight beats of the march. Even the trumpet call of the fourth is not notated in sixteenths, as tempting as this may have seemed:

Example 182

Thus, through the course of its rhythmical structure too, the tension of the *Appassionata* drama is led to its resolution.

The analogy of this architectural thinking to that of the *Pathétique* is too obvious to require any comment. But it is not confined to these two compositions. It represents rather the basic artistic idea, the spirit behind all Beethoven's works. Wherever we probe into his music, we find this same evolutional idea, whereby spirit is expressed through structure and structure becomes a spiritual phenomenon.*

* This very idea, this endeavour to create spiritual liberation through structural resolution, finds a unique expression in his last work, the String Quartet, Op. 135. (An analysis of this quartet, originally meant to follow the *Appassionata* analysis, is to be found in *The Thematic Process in Music*, pp. 206–18.)

12

The Problem of Form in
Beethoven's Music

1. TWO FORM-BUILDING FORCES IN MUSIC*

THERE are two form-building forces in music. The one, the inner force, consists of motivic action, the demonstration of which is the purpose of these analyses. The motifs, forming structural bricks, the substance of a composition, are combined into larger units—the patterns, from which the themes and thematic sections are developed in constant combinations and variations. The motifs also influence the modulations and the relationship between the sections; thus they even create the wider proportions through which form is brought about. Finally, an adequate evolution of these motivic elements enables the inspired composer to merge his structural ideas with spiritual and emotional ideas. This is heard dramatically in the motivic resolutions in the music of Beethoven.

However, in addition to this motivic flow which brings about the inner form of a musical work, there is also a second form-building force in music which models its outward shape. It is the method of grouping. To group, to divide and demarcate the continuous course of a work or a movement into parts and sections, is a natural means through which the shaping of a composition can be underlined and made easily recognizable for the listener.

In fact, many people, and among them some composers, are only aware of the second form-building force. The great composers, from the classical period right up to our time develop their compositional shapes primarily from the inner structure, though they often affirm this inner shaping through an outward grouping, so to speak.

---

* Cf. *The Thematic Process in Music*, pp. 109–38. Here the paragraphs above were expanded into a full chapter.

2. MEANS OF GROUPING

By what means can musical grouping be effected?

There are several; in fact all categories of musical expression contribute—harmony, rhythm, dynamics, etc. Moreover, some of these means of grouping originate in the motivic sphere. In what follows, we will enumerate the different means.

(i) MOTIVIC DIFFERENTIATION

Our method of analysis has demonstrated that in the course of a work, different motivic combinations—let us call them characters—are developed from the same motivic substance. Now if certain characters are limited to certain parts of a composition, as for instance in the *Pathétique*, where the *Allegro* up to a certain point contains exclusively characters such as:

Example 183

or related ones such as:

whereas characters of another type appear in the following part as:

then the listener will not fail to distinguish the two types as different architectural sections (in this case called the section of the first and second themes).

(ii) THEMATIC RESUMPTION

If, in the course of a work, certain shapes which have not been heard for some time are later resumed, then a concept of grouped parts will be created in the listener's mind. The part in which the shapes were heard first will be understood as an initial group, and the part in which the shapes are resumed will be conceived as a corresponding group.

If rightly placed, even a few notes can fulfil this role. When in the *Pathétique*, towards the end of the *Grave*, the shape:

Example 184

is resumed as a reiteration of the prime cell, then this minute shape, from which the concluding cadence leads to the tonic, is sufficient to make the whole *Grave* understood as a coherent unit of three parts. In a kind of transcribed application of the current terminology, we could thus well speak, within the *Grave*, of (1) an exposition, comprising the opening period, (2) a development, from the end of the opening period until:

and (3) a recapitulation, from the latter shape to the end.

However, not only tiny shapes but full thematic periods or sections are resumed, thus creating those large architectural shapes through which a movement is grouped into parts. In general, wherever one part of a composition is resumed, is recapitulated, after not having been heard for a time, then the two parts, the original and the one resumed, will be comprehended as corresponding sections. Through this, all these large divisions are brought about which the current terminology classifies as exposition, repetition, development, and recapitulation. This fact is too well known to every musician to require specific examples.

(iii) CADENCING HARMONIZATION

Furthermore, as every musician knows, one of the principal means of effecting musical grouping is the technique of harmonizing the compositional lines in cadences, that is to conclude them in the tonic or a substitute. This technique of grouping through cadencing is beyond the scope of our present analysis, and cannot be described here in detail. One specific point, however, should be stressed: harmonic shaping is not necessarily confined to the classical cadence, so well-known in the theoretical scheme. Any harmonic shaping, be it of a so-called 'polyphonic', or 'exotique', or of some other quality, may serve as an appropriate means of grouping, if only it can create a tonic or quasi-tonic impression.

Apart from motifs and harmonies the use of rhythm, dynamics, tempo and, in orchestral works, instrumentation—in short, all thinkable musical devices—may, by being applied in skilful differentiation, further support the effectiveness of the process of grouping. And last but not least, the whole phrasing and proportioning of the compositional course plays an important role, too. Let us recall for instance the ending of the first *Allegro* section of the *Pathétique*, where the last harmonic shaping (the interchange between tonic and dominant) is extended over no less than eight bars. Thus the most emphatic demarcation is achieved between this and the following section, even in anticipation, as it were:

Example 185

3. THE TYPE OF THE *PATHÉTIQUE*

The foregoing description of the means through which groups and sections are formed in music, may enable us to proceed to the wider problem of musical form.

For it is with regard to the amount to which these two form-building methods (the motifs and the grouping) participate in the shaping of the work, and especially with regard to the degree and manner in which the second method (the sectional grouping) is applied, that several phases of the compositional approach to musical form can be distinguished. In this respect the works of Beethoven analysed so far may well serve as fitting examples of the most typical of these phases.

The characteristic of that phase of musical form which is represented by the *Pathétique* lies in the fact that all these means of grouping just described are applied, and that they are applied in an accumulative way. Through this, an architectural picture of distinctly demarcated groups and sections emerges. For here all the devices work together, never against each other. The same sections which emerge from the harmonic shaping and phrasing are also distinguished through their motivic character, their specific rhythm and other attributes.

Although this creates a state of form of utter plasticity, therefore easily understandable, at the same time this state is also somewhat rigid and primitive. The richness and complexity of the structure of the *Pathétique* lies in the way in which the motivic connections are developed within the sections and from section to section, not in the merging of the groups and sections themselves. The sections are of course related to each other, they show analogy and contrast, but the sections as such are not yet alive in the *Pathétique*, they remain schematic.

Through this very fact, however, the type of the *Pathétique* is worthy of note for one more reason—that it represents the architectural phase which comes closest to the scheme that accepted theory has set up for musical form.

4. THE THEORETICAL SCHEME

This theoretical scheme of sonata form, or more generally the 'large' form as such, was developed according to the model of some early and rather simple sonatas in the beginning of the classical period. Its formal plan did not go much beyond the establishment of such general concepts as exposition, development, and recapitulation.

In addition, this theoretical scheme contains two specific features. First, it considers somewhat primitively, almost naively, the first period of a section as its 'theme'. Secondly, it states, as a kind of inherent though never explained rule, the presence of two themes in the exposition.* As an additional point, advanced through the theoretical scheme, the first of these two themes is regularly regarded as the main or principal theme, in comparison with which the other is classified as the secondary theme†

* The historic origin of modern sonata form has not yet been fully and convincingly clarified. That the theoretic view later put so much weight on the fact of two themes seems natural, considering that, compared with the scheme of one theme in preceding practice, the scheme of two themes had to appear as a progress. In the light of later compositional developments, however, the theory of two themes often appears obsolete (cf. 'The Role of Duothematicism in the Evolution of Sonata Form', Rudolph Réti, *Music Review*, Vol. XVLI, No. 2, May 1956).

† This holds true in strict analytical comment. But in the *Appassionata*, for instance, is not the principal theme of the *Allegro* the *third* section rather than the first?

—so that not only a succession, but a kind of quality in character and rank, is implied.

The first theme was envisaged as the strong, heroic one, the second as the more lyrical one. Moreover, having thus introduced the two leading themes as the backbone of the whole formal scheme, all the other parts had to be classified as annexes of these two. In this sense the terms entrata, bridge, coda, codetta, etc., were created as pointing to all the sections in between and around the two themes.

This rigid scheme of two themes and their sequels then remained, strangely enough, the extreme point to which the academic approach to form proceeded. Musical theory stubbornly clung to this scheme, and indulged in the most artificial explanations rather than adapt itself to compositional practice, which had long progressed far beyond. Beethoven's forms, for instance, are hardly ever limited to these two themes. Neither can the terms bridge, codetta and similar ones be fitted to his sonatas, since the groups to which they are usually applied often appear much too extended and weighted. They sometimes appear quite independent in an architectural sense, and would therefore seem to be shapes suggesting a third theme or at least a thematic section. At any rate, for these reasons, it seems in general more appropriate to speak of a first, a second and a third thematic section than of a theme as such in the works of Beethoven.

Though Beethoven's music, therefore, was never in complete conformity with any theoretical scheme, it is still true that the grouping of his earlier works, as for instance the *Pathétique*, showed a clear demarcation pointing to a leading first theme and a contrasting second theme. The prevailing conception accepts this, no matter whether or not an additional third section is included. Moreover, and this is the decisive point, this stage of the *Pathétique* shows not only thematic sections, but indeed real themes. Or, in other words, the first group of each section stands out in such symmetric plasticity, and is so distinctly demarcated as a unit, that it heads the whole section as a thematic example—and this is what we call a 'theme'.

5. THE TYPE OF THE *APPASSIONATA*

In the type of form which is represented by the *Appassionata*, the sectional division itself is perhaps no less distinct and transparent than in the preceding phase. However, the role which the thematic groups play, their distribution and equilibrium, are different.

As we know, there are, for instance, four different thematic groups in the exposition of the first movement of the *Appassionata*. But it would be just a matter of opinion to designate one of these four the principal theme, and more difficult still to decide which to regard as the secondary theme, or which group as a bridge. Not until after these four sections are heard does another small group follow, which, reiterating as it does the preceding shape in the obvious manner of a concluding cadence, could justly be classified as a kind of codetta. But the first four sections are too equal in importance to allow of any particular distinction between them. It would hardly seem satisfactory to proclaim, for instance, the first section in F minor as the principal theme and the emphatic third section in A flat major as the secondary one. The latter has not only too much weight for such a role, but more important, the two groups lack the decisive difference in character for such a classification. The group in A flat major appears as a varied intensification of the first theme rather than as a contrasting theme:

Example 186

section in F minor   section in A♭ major

Neither would it appear convincing to declare the second section, the one in E flat,* as the secondary theme. It, too, represents a varied reiteration of another part of the first section rather than a contrasting answer:

Example 187

from first section   section in E♭

And as for the fourth section, with the arpeggio motif sounding from its contour, the same situation prevails.

Thus, the first section, in relation to the following ones, almost assumes the character of an improvised introduction, an introduction somewhat analogous to the *Grave* in the *Pathétique*, though not marked as such; in the *Appassionata*, the tempo and rhythm of this 'introduction' are already those of the *Allegro*.

Yet on the other hand, all these four groups are much too different and independent to classify one of them as a bridge between the others. Owing to all this, the question of which theme is the principal one, and

[* Again, melodically speaking.—Ed.]

which the secondary, has to remain unanswered. In other words, in the *Appassionata*, in spite of its distinct grouping, the sections appear lifted from their schematic immovability; they are alive, and claim artistic value, not only for their content but also for their structural role as sections.

6. A THEMATIC CYCLE

Perhaps this new architectural spirit is felt still more strongly in the *Finale* of the *Appassionata*.

The *Finale*, too, spells out sonata form. Clearly the contour of an exposition, a development and a recapitulation takes shape. The exposition starts with that previously described introductory passage, whereafter a long thematic section follows. To be precise, we hear five groups, all with a homogeneous motivic phraseology, leaving no doubt that they have to be conceived as parts of one section. Still, it seems quite impossible to state which of these groups constitutes the theme, which the bridging parts. And here too, in following the theoretical scheme, it would seem specifically illogical to classify the first of these five groups as the principal theme. The first group (bars 20–28) is the most modest of all. In fact, the five groups gain step by step in value and weight, each forming an intensified expression of the foregoing thought. Specifically, the second group (bars 28–36) forms an increased replica of the first, while the fourth (bars 50–64) is a contrapuntal reiteration of the third (bars 36–50). The fifth group (bars 64–76) must probably be considered as only the first part of a longer annexe.

7. AN UNUSUAL REPETITION MARK

Not having been able to detect a group which clearly represents the theme in this first section, one might at least expect to find a contrasting secondary section. However, the bars which follow (bars 76–96) certainly cannot be classified as a second theme. Rather do they bear the character of an annexe, in relation to the preceding section. They affirm the evolution of this former section through some phrases which have the distinct flavour of a cadencing conclusion. They do not however build up a new thematic picture.

This first codetta is quickly followed by another which, resuming the shapes of the large first section in contrapuntal imitations, reveals the concluding, cadencing quality still more clearly (bars 96–112–117). It leads to that previously described interrupted cadence on the diminished seventh, out of which the development arises.

Thus we are now faced with the unusual sight of an exposition with only one thematic section plus a codetta.

However, within the ensuing development, as also described earlier, a new section emerges—one which, though naturally built from the old motifs, yet offers an independent, a new thematic picture:

Example 188

Obviously Beethoven felt the necessity of introducing such a new section, in order to avoid any overlong, enduring uniformity after the monothematic state of the exposition.

But through this procedure, a somewhat peculiar architectural situation arises—at least from the point of view of the analyst. For one might feel inclined to turn the whole schematic classification of the *Finale* around—that is to regard the part which in traditional theory is termed the development as the second thematic section of a huge exposition, formed by the old exposition plus the old development. Consequently, in this new classification the old exposition would shrink to a first thematic section, to which the old development would form the second section, while the old recapitulation would appear as the repetition after this new long exposition.

A chart renders this easily understandable:

Old Classification	Course of the Work	New Classification
Entrata	Introductory passages	Entrata
Exposition with one thematic section	First thematic section plus bridging groups	Exposition with two thematic sections
Development with new theme	Additional bridging groups plus another thematic section	Exposition with two thematic sections
Recapitulation	Reiteration of first thematic section plus bridging groups	Repetition
Coda	Presto	Coda

From a traditional aspect both these concepts appear somewhat unsatisfactory. For the one sets up an exposition with only one theme, whereas the second, while containing a second theme, lacks both the development and recapitulation, immediately jumping, as it were, to the coda.

As stated, it was doubtless to counteract this first insufficiency, namely the lack of a second theme, that Beethoven introduced that new theme into the development. But he obviously did not feel completely satisfied with the other architectural concept either. Now it can hardly be assumed that it was the lack of conformity with the theoretical scheme which bothered him. However, the spirit of form demands that any shape of importance will not be uttered without being repeated* sooner or later in the course of a composition—either literally or in variation, or at least in indication.

Just as a motif only acquires its structural sense—in fact only comes into existence—through reiteration, so in the same way sections formed through certain motivic characteristics (and these sections are called themes), have to be resumed or at least referred to later in the work. This reference, this resumption, will cause the listener to link these corresponding shapes and all others between them to an architectural unity. But without such a resumption, the sections of a work, even if distinctly grouped, do not appear as parts of a whole.

In this sense it is like a structural thorn in the flesh of the *Finale*, to have this new thematic section sound only once—no matter whether we consider it a new thought in the development or a second theme in a long exposition.

Therefore Beethoven, with the obvious desire of counteracting this deficiency, included a repetition mark at the end of the recapitulation before the coda. Such a repetition mark, not after the exposition, where it is normally to be seen, but after the recapitulation, certainly constitutes a rare event in the architectural realm of this era. It therefore drew an almost unanimous cry of surprise, not to say of objection, from the commentators. In fact, many editors bluntly advise the performer to ignore it, as it renders the work overlong (see for instance the von Bülow edition). However, the reason that Beethoven considered it necessary was the fact, so understandable from an architectural aspect, that it was distasteful to him to have this lonely little theme floating helplessly around. Only by repetition did this theme, too, become a part of the higher architectural entity of the sonata. It is this entity we call form.†

* Cf. *Tonality—Atonality—Pantonality*, Rudolph Réti. Rockliff, London; Macmillan, New York; p. 95.

† Admittedly, from a dramatic point of view, this literal repetition makes the piece too long. This might indicate a slight weakness on Beethoven's part. What probably should have been done was to repeat the part in a reduced and varied form. However, there is no point in going into the matter at this time.

8. FORM IN THE LAST QUARTETS

In Beethoven's final phase, motivic evolution becomes almost the sole structural force. True, the general features of the theoretical scheme, as defined in the concept of exposition, development and recapitulation, are still recognizable here too. But apart from this, architectural grouping is reduced to a minimum. As we may recall in the quartet Op. 135,* a small phrase rather than a full period constitutes the thematic pattern of the composition—i.e. the motivic combination from which its shapes are formed. Thus to a certain extent motivic characterization has even taken over the role of the themes, which, at least in the first movement, are hardly visible as distinctly demarcated groups. For though we see grouped phrases of one, two or three bars, which through repetition and variation assume the quality of thematic shapes, we seldom discover full periods of one homogenous character, from which whole sections are developed. In the current terminology only such periods would be called themes. As for the sectional division, it is sometimes audible, but often, it would seem, intentionally obscured rather than emphasized.

9. STYLE

Two architectural forces, as was said earlier, are to be distinguished in music. One force, working from within the structural depths—the force of the motifs and motivic connections—develops the themes as well as both the thematic continuity and thematic contrast. The second force, the method of sectional dividing and grouping, forms the architectural surface of a composition.

As already hinted, the proportion to which these two forces participate in the building of a musical composition determines the degree to which this composition can be fitted into the concept of form according to accepted theory. Since this theory omits motivic structure in its aspect of a form-building force, taking cognizance only of the second force—the method of grouping—the following situation arises.

The first phase of form, as represented in the *Pathétique*, is that which almost conforms to the theoretical picture. Since, in such works, the difference in the motivic characters is clearly wrought in the groups and sections, and since these sections also indicate the accepted scheme of two contrasting themes—and especially since the leading groups of the sections are really shaped in the plasticity and symmetry of 'themes' from which the sections are developed—these earlier works of Beethoven

---

* Cf. *The Thematic Process in Music*, pp. 206–18.

can easily be regarded as approximate models of the theoretical design.

Works from the next phase, however, represented by the *Appassionata*, may hardly be considered such models. The conventional theoretical view would probably fit them into this scheme, but in so doing, it would have to declare many of their architectural features to be exceptions, individual deviations from their original nature. Thus the usual terms, such as first or second theme, bridge, etc., would here be applied in an inaccurate, incongruous way.

In the last phase, that of the string quartet, Op. 135, only some general indications of the theoretical picture such as exposition, recapitulation, etc., remain alive; in most of its architectural detail not more than traces of the old scheme are to be discovered. To be sure, in this type too, one may still point out different thematic groups and sections, but they often melt into one another, both as sectional units and in their motivic characterization. In fact, in some parts of this type of composition, no sectional design becomes audible at all.

Having demonstrated how Beethoven, in the course of his development as a composer, turned more and more to that inner force of motivic architecture as his form-building device, one should by no means assume that any less artistic value is to be placed on that other structural force, sectional division. True motivic structure is the all-permeating element from which the real content and architecture of a musical work arises. But whether, and to what degree, a composer wishes to make this architecture easily understandable through grouping and sectional demarcation, has nothing to do with the artistic level of a work whatsoever. Rather is it a matter of his individual way of expression, producing the specific style in which the composer wishes to set forth his musical thoughts and feelings.

Beethoven, in the course of his life's work, shows a unique evolution from a style of sharp, transparent sectional demarcation to one where the groups and sections pass smoothly into one another, sometimes even overlapping or melting into one another. Thus they are no longer comprehensible as independent units at all.

Section 3
Thematic Architecture

13

Architectural Planning

IN the preceding analyses the different methods have been described through which, on the basis of thematic structure, the whole composition is built. The main points of this technique may be recapitulated as follows:

(1) *Motivic Unity:* meaning that the content of a composition is formed from one motivic material.

(2) *Thematic Consistency:* demonstrating that the motifs are combined into larger units, so that such a combination forms the pattern according to which all the groups and especially the decisive thematic groups of a work are modelled.

(3) *Architectural Planning:* pointing to the method of shaping the motifs and themes from the beginning in such a way that, by transforming them in an appropriate manner as the work progresses, and finally leading them to a resolution, a kind of story or 'architectural plot' is evolved which makes all the shapes of a composition a part and expression of one higher unity.

Of these three techniques—which in practice, naturally, are not as distinctly differentiated as in our theoretical enumeration, but merge into one another—the first two form the backbone of the structural technique. But technique (3) is perhaps the most remarkable of all, since it is through architectural planning that the last and highest form of a musical work is brought about.

The foregoing chapter described how the outward form of a composition is shaped through the technique of grouping. It explained how, by means of the resumption of groups and sections, a feeling of architectural unity is created, which makes the compositional course appear in the listener's mind as a whole. This is the well-known structural method of repetition or recapitulation.

However, in *architectural resumption* the inner and outer form-building forces in music actually meet, and their correlating influence becomes transparently clear. For although resumption makes a composition appear as a unity—although, if a theme is introduced and then repeated on a later occasion the ear will comprehend this course as a 'form'—yet, unless this form is filled with a structural idea of evolution it will remain a hollow shell. The listener would realize that such a work, though having a sort of architectural logic and symmetry, still lacks any inner progress and enrichment. Pure resumption, that is the mere placing of corresponding sections side by side, would create a static feeling. That is why outward resumption has to be complemented by an inner development. We call such inner development 'architectural planning' and we observed it in our preceding analysis through those small yet decisive motivic alterations which lead a work to its final solution.

Let us recall the *Appassionata* again. A small particle, reading:

Example 189

(a)

was the basic figure which in numerous differently phrased variations spread throughout the whole first movement, structurally, as the main idea. In the analysis this particle was called the prime cell, and around it all the larger shapes and groups of the movement were found to be centred.

By altering this figure slightly, another little shape came to life:

(b)

from which the solemn mood of the *Andante* was produced.

These two versions of the prime cell:

Example 190

(a) representing the *Allegro* and (b) the *Andante*

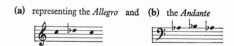

were then taken over in the third movement, in a new phrasing, as:

Example 191

version (a)—first *Finale* theme:

version (b)—second *Finale* theme:

or combined in one shape:

But not until in the *Presto* coda of the *Finale* did a last variant of the cell emerge:*

Example 192

At this point a definite resolution of the work is achieved—a resolution equally convincing both architecturally and emotionally.

Such minute alterations as these:

Example 193

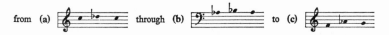

might at first appear negligible and hardly worthy of mention; nevertheless, by observing their effect and structural consequences within the composition, it would seem that they form the very phenomenon through which the great architectural plot, the innermost artistic idea of the *Appassionata* is brought to life.

Similarly, in the *Pathétique*, the original combination:

[* See my footnote on p. 118.—ED.]

(d)

is altered in the last movement to:

(e)

and this minute alteration is decisive in the plan of the work. For by building the *Finale* theme thus:

Example 194

(a)

in contrast to the *Grave*:

(b)

and by maintaining the characteristic phrasing throughout all the shapes of the *Finale* (bringing fourths and fifths constantly into the picture)—an architectural and emotional 'plot' is brought to life as the highest artistic expression of the work.

In the following analyses our attention will be focused mainly on the ways in which the final resolution of a composition is achieved. It will be necessary, however, to use motivic fundamentals as the starting point from which the higher architectural ideas can be traced.

14
The Thematic Pitch of the
Kreutzer Sonata

1. *INTRODUCTION* AND *PRESTO*

BEETHOVEN'S Sonata for Violin and Piano, Op. 47, the so-called *Kreutzer* Sonata, represents a striking example of the way in which the magnificent structure and emotional strength of a work stem from the ingenious evolution and variation of one basic thematic idea. For this very reason, however, in order to understand the higher architectural scheme, we must first become clear about the fundamental thematic material from which it was developed. Let us accordingly follow the first thematic line in the *Presto*★ of the sonata's opening movement:

Example 195

We may divide this shape into three segments, as indicated by the brackets in the example. We will call segment I the *prime shape* and subdivide it into two corresponding *particles, a* and *b*:

Example 196

These particles naturally appear at times as *inversions*:

★ The first movement of the sonata will henceforth be referred to as *Introduction* and *Presto*, the second as *Andante*, the third as *Finale*.

Also, their accidentals sometimes appear changed for melodic reasons: thus F natural to E may appear as F sharp to E, or G sharp to A as G natural to A.

On closer examination, segment II turns out to be a derivative of segment I, and in essence merely a stepwise sequence of the initial particle (see Example 197). In this sequence, however, a kind of pedal is included, first on E, then on A, through which Beethoven's score is brought to life. Thus the motivic content of segment II may be reduced to a stepwise ascent henceforth called the *step-ladder* and a motif of note-repetition, henceforth referred to as the *E and A pedals*:

Example 197

Segment III is a combination of an ascending fourth and a falling third and will be known as the 4+3. It appears both in inversion (falling fourth and ascending third) and in reversion (3+4 instead of 4+3).

Having established the motivic fundamentals, we may now outline the *thematic pattern* of the *Kreutzer* Sonata. It is formed by a combination of three motivic elements: *prime shape plus step-ladder plus* 4+3. To these we add one characteristic feature, the importance of which will be demonstrated later, the *two pedals E and A*.

(i) THE *INTRODUCTION*

The sonata begins with a slow *Introduction*. This Introduction divulges a very interesting psychological structural idea: namely a kind of *search for the prime shape*—or, to be precise, for the prime shape at that pitch which later turns out to have been the 'original' one; that is, the pitch heard in the beginning of the *Presto* theme. Or in other words, the *Introduction* is a search for the two prime particles, E to F and G sharp to A. Let us see whether Beethoven's score confirms this statement.

The *Introduction* opens with an improvisational exclamation by the violin:

Example 198

The lower voice with which this phrase begins, shows the 4+3 (the fourth A to D followed by a series of falling thirds); while the upper voice, consisting of a series of falling thirds plus a rising fourth, spells the motif in reversion, 3+4. Then one of the prime particles (G sharp to A) appears for the first time, and after another ascending fourth is followed by a corresponding particle (D to C sharp).

Thus a first provisional expression of the main shape is achieved; namely, *a pair of corresponding particles*, though at this point only one of them, G sharp to A, is heard at that pitch which will later prove to be the decisive one.

Following this, the piano repeats the improvisional exclamation. Significantly, however, one note has been changed, F sharp into F natural—significantly, because through this the violin, by taking over the F natural, has an opportunity of spelling the other prime particle also at the (final) original pitch,[*] though still in inversion (F to E):

Example 199

Now the piano suggests a new pitch for the corresponding particle, E to D sharp:

Example 200

It is not accepted—the violin insists on A to G sharp, from which a meaningful *crescendo* restores the original G sharp to A:

[*] Cf. *The Thematic Process in Music.*

147

Example 201

whereafter, again, another pitch, this time C to B, is attempted:

Example 202

With this, after a series of inversions, the definite phrasing of the coming prime shape is ascertained. What follows is the search for the final pitch—a search so obvious, and so transparent, that few similar examples can be found in music.

Let us become clearly aware of the situation. One of the particles, G sharp to A, is already firmly established. Now the improvisor-composer hunts for the other. He first tries C sharp to D—that is, the inversion of one of the particles from the opening bars, linking it to the newly won C natural to B:

Example 203

Then he suggests B flat instead of B natural:

Still not satisfied, he tries at last E to F, which had already emerged in the beginning but had then disappeared. Now, however, it is finally accepted as the definite pitch. For the composer sounds this E to F once, twice . . . eight times:

Example 204

The introductory improvisation has reached its goal. The actual work can now begin.

(ii) THE *PRESTO*

A pair of corresponding particles has been established as the work's first thematic utterance. However, in this composition, it is not only the motifs as such, but the motifs at a certain pitch which are to prove decisive. Indeed, the whole structure of the sonata is, so to speak, socketed in this thematic pitch. E to F plus A to G sharp forms the foundation from which the entire sonata is developed. To prove this and to demonstrate through it certain decisive aspects of Beethoven's creative method, is the purpose of this study.

After having been heard once, the *Presto* theme is repeated, but this time with the piano in the leading role, the violin being subdued to a charming contrapuntal imitation:

Example 205

Then a new group enters:

Example 206

What is the content of this new shape, which—as we look at it more closely—becomes increasingly interesting?

We must become conscious of what an unusual melodic line this example represents. It is hardly a 'period' in the traditional sense, nor even a 'melody'. Rather, it again expresses a kind of improvisational progression, a search—a search for what? Obviously, again a search for that basic figure we called the prime shape. Starting from E to F (the first particle) it climbs (thus including the second motivic element, the 'step-ladder') to G flat, to G natural, with the *sforzati* revealing the excitement as the goal is neared. And with G sharp to A, the goal has been reached, for this is the second particle. Now, with a cadencing phrase in the characteristic *Kreutzer* accent, the group is concluded.

This example reveals much of the mystery of Beethoven's creative method. Musical minds have often asked themselves 'How do composers find their lines? Wherein lies the secret of melodic creation?' The *Kreutzer* Sonata shows that certain psychic urges, connected with a work's thematic fundamentals, account in great part for what appears to the listener as 'musical flow'. The outcry of the two particles is indeed the innermost impulse which brought the above melodic line to life.

The *sforzati* in the example above also appear simultaneously in the piano part, and one might well wonder whether here they are not meaningless in a structural, that is in a thematic sense as the line proceeds differently in the piano. However, surprisingly enough, here they spell the other prime element, the $4+3$ (in contrary motion): B flat, D, A:

Example 207

A section follows which in its network of accentuated figurations forms, from a dramatic aspect, one of the characteristic stimuli of the sonata. Structurally these shapes are only of bridging value and are but concluding harmonies devoid of thematic progression; yet it may be worth noting that even these cadencing bridges stress the thematic pitch of the prime shape, G sharp to A and F to E, though the F natural is in one instance altered to F sharp:

Example 208

The next substantial group is then formed, in bars 61–67:

Example 209

And here the spectacle continues. For this whole group is again an utterance of the prime shape—the prime shape at original pitch. The two corresponding particles (*a* and *b*)—the G sharp for melodic reasons smoothed to G natural—clearly form the structural backbone, emphasized particularly through Beethoven's *sforzati*. Besides this main content, another pair of corresponding particles (*c* and *d*) appears interpolated.

Not until after this does the prime shape appear *for the first time at a transposed pitch* (as G to F sharp plus D sharp to E), with the second particle prolonged through several repetitions:

Example 210

Through this, the first section of the great exposition is brought to a conclusion, and the second theme follows.

This theme (Example 211), one of the most beautiful, most 'Beethovenian' cantilenas given us by the great composer, forms the utmost contrast, in mood and character, to the lines of the first section. Thus it is highly impressive to note how its design again contains the prime thought, and is indeed based on the idea of a *contrapuntal combination of the two prime particles* (the F of the second particle 'melodized'* to F sharp):

Example 211

But let us examine the course of the full theme more closely.

As we see, in the opening group the bass line of the first four bars represents the 4+3, while the melody in the soprano part (the violin line) develops from G sharp to A, to which in a kind of contrary motion G sharp to F sharp answers.

Such a formation of the thematic melody from one of the basic motifs conforms with the general concept of structural logic. As a continuation, however, one might expect a somewhat new melodic thought. But the following phrase (bars 5–8 in Example 211) is by no means a new thought: it is essentially a repetition of the first, although slightly enlarged by the inclusion of a suspension on the B. To be precise, it is a twofold repetition. For the turn on the G sharp, once resolved, also yields a repetition of the first phrase:

Example 212

Moreover, a further repetition (thus virtually the third) follows in the next bars, now omitting the turn:

Example 213

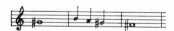

* Cf. 'Identical Pitch and Change of Accidentals' in *The Thematic Process in Music*, pp. 100–105.

With this, the first part of the theme is brought to a close, and we have to admit that this line hardly represents a truly shaped 'melody', the kind of melody which according to all traditional concepts we might expect a 'theme' to be. It is little more than a melismatic phrase several times repeated, though it is shaped into a half-close by harmonic demarcation. The second part of the theme proves this idea all the more clearly. For after this somewhat problematic first half, one might expect the second half to emerge as a truly new melodic shape answering the first. But nothing of the sort. For it is indeed a reduced—a still more reduced—reiteration in the minor of the first half:

Example 214

Now to every musical mind this 'second theme' of the *Kreutzer* is treasured as a particularly beautiful musical utterance. Therefore, since our faith in its artistic value is probably stronger than any theoretical schematism, we shall doubtless, having the choice between practice and theory, choose the former. Thus this interesting theme *is only one more proof that musical melody, in fact musical form, is brought about through an improvisational, almost psychological process rather than according to any traditional concept or formula.*

And since we shall be forced to abandon still other cherished concepts in the ensuing part of the exposition, it seems quite understandable that analysts should have avoided commenting thoroughly on the *Kreutzer*. For the next part does not form, as might be expected, a new section which would be the third in the exposition, but rather it seems to be *a continuation of the first section*—as is suggested by its tempo and whole character.

Thus, an unusual scheme of form emerges from the exposition; *one long thematic section interrupted by a second theme.* Or charted:

(A) part one of first thematic section,

(B) second theme,

(C) part two of first thematic section.

We see a *third theme* evolve in this last section of the exposition, representing the culmination, so to speak, of all the former thematic shapes of the *Presto*:

Example 215

In an uncannily transparent way this theme shows again that, with Beethoven, melodic invention arose as a magical combination of thematic and psychic impulses—or, in other words, that he expressed his emotions in extremely clear-cut structural forms. Thematically, the first five bars of this theme are, of course, a clear sequence of 'particles' lifted in step-ladder form to the octave, and followed by a variant of the 4 + 3. Yet one feature which was not present in the initial *Presto* theme is now included. It is one of the fundamental elements of the *second theme*: *the turn*. Compare the turn from the second theme (Example 216(a)) with the third *Presto* shape (Example 216(b)):

Example 216

(a)

(b)

Thus, this third theme is in its structural core *an expanded variant of the first theme plus a characteristic element from the second theme*—an architectural idea both fascinating and logical.

Of one feature, however, we have almost lost sight—the expression of the two prime particles at original pitch. In this third theme it seems indeed to have vanished from the picture. However, while the piano plays the third theme, the violin enters with a few pizzicato chords. These pizzicato accents in the violin often constitute a problematic point in the performance of the *Kreutzer*. Separated by rests, and forming discords with the melodic line of the theme, they usually pass by as, so to speak, isolated sound effects, to which neither the performer nor the listener attribute much real meaning. Yet understood as a connected unit they represent a quite logical musical utterance: a 'period', clearly divided into two halves (see Example 215). The first half, no doubt, centres on the prime particle at original pitch, F to E, to which the second half adds one of those concluding cadences with which almost all the melodic lines of the *Kreutzer* end.

Where, however, is the second particle, A to G sharp, to be found? At this point the musician is faced with an interesting situation. If, he might argue, thematic structure truly represents a compositional principle, then the second particle, the A to G sharp, must—indeed, *must*—be seen somewhere in the vicinity of the first. Failing to discover it immediately, he might for one moment feel like the astronomer who, in plotting, had located a new planet which his telescope for the time being failed to reveal. But in music, just as in astronomy, the search continues; and suddenly an unusual formation catches the eye:

Example 217

Here the particle is clearly to be seen, if only we connect the A of the violin with the G sharp of the piano, with which it clashes in a wondrous discord. Thus both particles, the whole thematic unit, are at work again in the third theme.

Should anyone consider these explanations to be artificial, he might note that a strikingly similar idea can be traced in the preceding group. In the midst of this preceding group the following dissonances emerge:

Example 218

Here we find again the phenomenon of the two particles at original pitch. But while in the third theme E to F is heard as a melodic phrase followed by G sharp to A as a clashing discord, in the present example the pattern is precisely reversed: particle *b*, G sharp to A, appears in the melodic line (the bass), while E to F sounds as a violent discord in the soprano part. Such corresponding schemes in two successive groups cannot be taken as a mere play of chance, they must be rooted in intentional shaping—particularly since violent discords like those just quoted are such striking features, striking even for Beethoven, rejoice though he did in dissonance.

Indeed the G sharp in the piano part of the third theme was long felt to be so disturbing a discord, beyond all traditional conceptions, that many editors hesitated to recognize it, and blithely and arbitrarily changed the G sharp to G natural. However, see Breitkopf und Hartel *Kritische Gesamtausgabe*, where the original text is preserved.

2. THE *ANDANTE*

Turning from the *Presto* to the next movement, the *Andante con Variazioni*, we become aware that the architectural pitch not only continues, but forms the very basis of an astonishing relationship between the first and second movements. For since the first movement, viewed harmonically as an architectural whole, must be considered as A minor, it would seem to represent the second prime particle, A to G sharp; thus, there remains for the *Andante*, if the whole prime shape is to be completed, no other choice than to represent an expression of the other particle, E to F. In the first place, the key of the second movement has to be F—which is indeed the case; but more than that, just as the *Presto* ended with the particle G sharp to A, the *Andante* now begins with the other particle, F to E:

Example 219

Ending of first movement   Beginning of second movement

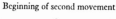

A more illuminating example of the all-permeating thematic spirit of Beethoven's structural thinking can hardly be imagined.

Moreover, while the two particles in the example above spell the prime shape as a link *between* the two movements, each also forms part of a full prime shape *within* its own respective movement. This is seen in the *Presto*, in the fact that before the concluding stretto, which is centred on G sharp to A, a few *Adagio* bars are interpolated (Example 220)—emphasizing for a moment the corresponding particle E to F, before concluding with A to G sharp:

Example 220

As for the *Andante* theme itself, it is built on this same idea of corresponding particles, as seen in the fact that the two halves of both periods of the theme begin with the two particles in an amazingly symmetrical interchange: the two halves of the first period are directed by F to E and G sharp to A respectively, those of the second by A to G natural and F to E:

Example 221

First period

Example 222

Second period

The further motivic detail of the theme consists of the step-ladder, the 4+3, and the turn, as shown by the brackets.*

3. THE *FINALE*

After all that we have experienced in the first two movements, we might well expect the same picture to evolve in the *Finale*, possibly

[*Réti ignores the variations, for the obvious reason given in his section on the *Andante* of the *Appassionata*: 'The variations, as almost literal repetitions of the theme, require no detailed analysis'.—ED.]

intensified. However, we look in vain for the prime shape at original pitch—it seems to have disappeared. To be precise, A to G sharp still flickers from the score, but E to F seems to have become wholly obscured.

What has happened?

As in all of Beethoven's works when they draw to a conclusion, an *architectural resolution* has taken place. In brief, the original pattern:

Example 223

has been replaced by a slightly modified one:

Example 224

or in other words, the original motivic idea of the *Kreutzer* Sonata appears in the *Finale* transformed into an expression of the dominant-tonic. No longer E to F plus A to G sharp, but a phrase formed by D sharp to E plus G sharp to A, has become the prime shape in the *Finale*.

This new prime shape, these new particles, are immediately heard at the opening of the *Finale* in a contrapuntal setting:*

Example 225

They are also heard in the ensuing theme, which, however, does not correspond to the lyrical second theme of the first movement, but might better be termed an offspring of the first movement's third theme.

[*G sharp to A appears inverted, in Réti's example; but an alternative interpretation would show it in direct form, in rhythmic counterpoint with D sharp to E, and fused with the 4+3 as 3+4 (Réti indicates this latter element himself in Example 232). The example here is mine.—ED.]

This theme, too, spells the new prime shape, the first of its four groups expressing D sharp to E, the last one G sharp to A. In fact it constitutes one of the rare cases in Beethoven's music where a theme of one movement is almost verbally (even though only in part) repeated in another movement. Compare:

Theme of first movement

Example 226

with *Finale* theme

Still, this *Finale* theme fails to recall one important feature of the later part of the *Presto* theme, namely the aforementioned *turn* from the lyric theme. However, this recollection is reiterated in the next, the 'secondary' and quasi-lyrical theme of the *Finale*:

Example 227

The second half of this shape centres on the turn, while the first half is formed by a variant of the 4 + 3. And it certainly constitutes a striking parallelism that the 'secondary second themes' of both the first movement and the *Finale* feature the *turn* as their most characteristic melodic feature. However, the theme is also interesting for other reasons, as it suddenly sounds in a 2/4 rhythm instead of the general 6/8 of the *Finale*. Such an interruption, unusual in Beethoven's time, might perhaps be explained merely as an impressive way of raising this charming theme to prominence within its own environment. But why, then, does Beethoven again interrupt this new rhythm by inserting one bar of the old 6/8 ? He certainly does not do it for the purpose of keeping the 6/8 latently alive throughout the 2/4, but rather for a strikingly impressive architectural reason—namely, to make the new prime shape all the more emphatically audible:

Example 228

The composer's consciousness of the phenomenon is not to be doubted—each time, precisely at the moment when the change in rhythm and dynamic takes place, the resolved prime shape is sounded. And at the very point when the 6/8 is definitely restored, the predominating A to G sharp gives way to an emphatic D sharp to E in the violin:

Example 229

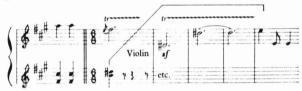

Now, as a resumé, a thematic chart of the sonata would read:

Example 230

Presented in this schematic way, these particles may look rather meagre. But envisaged as musical keystones from which the whole design of the work is built, they stand forth in all their importance as the true architectural plot of the *Kreutzer* Sonata.

To make the work's great architectural plan fully understood a few further considerations should be added. First, the scheme just described has to be broadened. While we have said that the original prime particle E to F was changed in the *Finale* into D sharp to E, it must now be added that a variant of this D sharp to E also becomes audible, which reads D natural to C sharp. In other, more appropriate words, the resolution of the original prime shape takes place in the *Kreutzer* in two alternative versions:

Example 231

Both versions are of course expressions of a dominant-tonic phenomenon. And this new variant of the prime shape has not been introduced
simply to enable the analyst to fit one more shape from Beethoven's
score into his chart: the presence of the two variants is, as will be demonstrated presently, a real and intentional part of the architectural plan of
the work. Both variants are established emphatically from the very
beginning of the *Finale*. As if wishing to stress that the old prime shape
has ceased to exist, the composer introduces the two variants, which are
to replace it. Thus the opening of the *Finale* reads:

Example 232

and the opening of this theme's second group:

Example 233

The first chord might be considered an 'echo in miniature' of the
Introduction from the first movement. Then the two variants follow—
D sharp to E sounding from the first group, D natural to C sharp from
the second, each particle accompanied by the corresponding particle
G sharp to A on the piano.* Therefore, in each case, the full prime shape
has come into existence.

[* See my note on p. 158.—ED.]

This motivic spelling of the two variants continues throughout the whole *Finale*. The 'second' theme, for instance, expresses variant *a* as was previously demonstrated; but the reiteration of this theme in the recapitulation expresses variant *b*.

Now we understand why both variants, D sharp to E and C sharp to D, were heard (in inversion) in the work's *Introduction*:

Example 234

They are the future *Finale* variants, *a* and *b*, and through them the later resolution is presaged.

Thus in the *Kreutzer*, from the beginning, a definite pitch* plays an essential part in shaping the structure of the work. And this idea of an overall pitch is intensified through one last feature which only a mind like Beethoven's could carry to such heights. This feature has its origin in *the two pedals on E and A*, which first emerged in the opening theme of the *Presto* (see Example 197). The first of the two pedals, the one on E, sounds through the whole exposition of the *Presto* as a main characteristic of all three themes of the first movement:

Example 235

(a) *First theme* (piano part):

(b) *Second theme* (first group)—first from the piano part (soprano and tenor):

(c) *Second theme* (second group)—violin part:

*For a discussion of pitches emerging within the keys, see *The Thematic Process in Music*, pp. 222–23: also 'Tonality through Pitches', pp. 76–79, in the author's *Tonality—Atonality—Pantonality*.

(d) *Third theme*—(note Beethoven's *sforzati*):

Besides, the pedal shines out from almost every corner of the score, for instance:

Example 236

In the recapitulation, it is only natural that the A pedal becomes predominant, although the E pedal does not by any means fade from the picture. In fact, these architectural pedals sound through the whole movement like an immovable axis; and around this axis the other shapes are grouped, partly in support of, partly in collision with it: a giant expression of the dominant-tonic phenomenon to which the whole work finally drives.

In the *Andante*, since the key is F, this phenomenon has to remain somewhat subdued. Yet at the climax of its last variation, a line of trills emerges, leading to the prime shape:

Example 237

Also note how the *fermata* in the piano part is not put on the first note, but on the second, the 'thematic' G sharp.

And in the *Finale*, the E and the A pedals are again spelled out through the *sforzati* in a highly impressive shaping in the opening period:

Example 238

Before the recapitulation enters, we hear the E once more in the long whisper of the violin's *pianissimo*:

Example 239

In the coda it again cries from the heights of the violin in *sforzati*, while the piano thunders the corresponding G sharp to A:

Example 240

And this E pedal, finally resolved in the tonic, concludes the work. In the example below, note the dynamics in general and the almost simultaneous three *sforzati* on the E's of the first measure.

Example 241

15

The Thematic Model of the
Waldstein Sonata

A QUITE different type of architectural planning becomes visible in the Piano Sonata, Op. 53, the *Waldstein*. The main characteristic of this structure is that all its themes are built from the same model with a uniformity not often found in a large musical work.

At first thought this might seem no novelty. In our preceding analyses we have already experienced the generating power of the thematic pattern—that is, a certain motivic combination from which all the groups of a composition were formed. Yet in the *Waldstein* this principle seems to be considerably intensified: its themes appear not only as images of the same thematic idea, but practically as replicas of one model theme. The extent to which this analogy is developed in the *Waldstein* is certainly unusual in musical architecture, and makes this sonata one of the structural wonders in Beethoven's work.

The model is simple. It is the stepwise ascent or descent from tonic to dominant, to which a small phrase, a loop, is annexed. The tonic and the dominant are the two accentuated centres from which the loop leads back again.

The main theme of the *Rondo-Finale* reads:*

Example 242

By changing this line to the minor and transposing it a half tone higher, we hear:

Example 243

which is synonymous with the second theme of the *Allegro*:

* The first movement is referred to as the *Allegro,* the second as the *Adagio,* the third as the *Rondo.*

Example 244

Here the loop is added in a separate phrase, reading:

Example 245

It is interesting to note that the tonic-dominant relation is still immanent in the melodic line, which, however, through a new harmonization, acquires a different meaning and flavour.

By placing the shape in contrary motion, another theme of the sonata is produced—the second theme of the *Rondo*:

Example 246

In another case, a similar leading upwards from the tonic to the dominant, the first *Allegro* theme comes to life:

Example 247

Here the loop is, as seen above, extended first over only three notes, but then in a repetition expanded to five notes (the full compass of the tonic-dominant).

The basic idea is also clearly visible in the theme of the *Adagio*:

Example 248

and also in the last remaining theme, the third of the *Rondo*:

Example 249

This theme represents the most interesting variety of all. For though the original model is clearly recognizable, the accentuated dominant appears shifted through a kind of syncopation to the second eighth note —and, by the way, this syncopated accent on the weak beat is very effective in performance.

The full theme is then brought into being through a threefold repetition of this shape, each shape being repeated a fourth higher than the preceding. In this way the dominant-tonic idea is spelled through a sequencing progression:

Example 250

Having demonstrated the growth of the themes from a basic model, we may now follow the wider architectural course of the work. The opening theme, after its first appearance in C, is repeated a tone lower in B flat:

Example 251

However, no real exposition is yet developed from this beginning. For in continuing, the loop is simply resolved into a series of passages which soon fall to a pause. Through this, the whole section assumes the quality of one of those 'searching attempts', so familiar to us from other works—although this time it is not a search for the theme, which has already been established, but rather for a definite form of the exposition.

This definite form is found when in the following the whole beginning is repeated, but now the reiterated theme is led up to D (instead of down to B flat):

Example 252

From here, by resolving the loop again into a group of passages and figurations, a full section is developed, which finally flows into the second theme—the structural content of which was built from the basic model, as has already been described. It, too, is followed by a series of figurations formed through constantly interchanging tonics and dominants:

Example 253

The figurations, now developed into a huge arc, fill the whole section. The effect which they emanate is proof that a great composer can evolve an impressive structure from a simple foundation, merely through his art of phrasing and the maintenance of one convincing style.

In this way the tonic-dominant model permeates the whole work. There is hardly a more transparent expression thinkable than that formed by those mysterious particles in the famous introduction to the recapitulation:

Example 254

or through shapes such as:

Example 255

In the second case the loop in miniature is also included.

These two shapes, by the way, appear successively as augmentations in a significant counterpoint to the second theme (the figurations are added almost in the way of a motet):

Example 256

In accordance with all this, the tonic-dominant phenomenon also becomes the main harmonic force in the sonata, and it is especially interesting, from the point of view of this analysis, to observe that it also forms the greater part of the work's modulations.

A few of these examples follow. They show the development both of the *Allegro* and the *Rondo* in constant dominant-tonic progressions from group to group (C to F to B flat, etc.):

Example 257

Development of Allegro

Development of Rondo

Thus having registered the main structural features of the *Waldstein,* the remaining problem would seem to be the type of resolution through which its architectural plot is formed. This resolution is the plainest thinkable. The thematic groups which in the *Allegro* join the corresponding groups in the harmonic progression,

Example 258

either one tone lower:

or one tone higher:

are in the *Rondo* simply joined as pairs, consisting of the tonic group and dominant group:

Example 259

Continued overleaf.

Let us become clear about this. Each of the two groups of the theme, being derivatives of that basic model from which all the themes of the work are formed, is itself a progression from the tonic to the dominant. The resolution, however, consists in the fact that in the *Rondo* the first group, viewed as a whole, represents the tonic (though formed by a tonic plus a dominant). To this, the second group, representing the dominant, is added (in the first movement the groups followed each other from C to B flat or from C to D). This is clearly expressed through the corner notes of the harmonies, C and G, in the bass. The particular importance Beethoven attributed to it is seen in the fact that he added pedal precisely in accordance with the concept just described. The pedal notation seen in the example is Beethoven's.

Thus, in the *Waldstein* the architectural plot is brought about simply by connecting two thematic groups in a tonic-dominant relation. Those more complicated motivic alterations, which represent the dramatic tension and resolution of other works of Beethoven, are omitted here. Architecturally —and probably emotionally as well—the *Waldstein* lives, so to say, on a plane rather than in space. Its symmetric, serene simplicity flows into the pastoral *Rondo*—although this pastoral quality rises to a triumphant mood in the second and third *Rondo* themes. The sonata concludes with the call of the cuckoo, first in *pianissimo*, then in jubilant *fortissimo*:

Example 260

It is the sound of the cuckoo which we recognize from another great pastoral work of Beethoven. Motivically, however, this cry of the cuckoo is a replica of the first particle of the first *Rondo* theme:

Example 261

or the inversion of the first *Allegro* theme:

Example 262

No change of the original motivic substance takes place in the Waldstein.

To complete its structural picture, one more feature may be described. It refers to the basic thematic model from which its architecture is built. This model is regularly introduced by a kind of *auftakt* (up-beat)—a motivic *auftakt*, so to say, which is not necessarily always an *auftakt* in a rhythmical sense. The first *Rondo* theme, for instance, leaps from C to its actual melodic line:

Example 263

Analogously, the second *Rondo* theme rises from these two preceding E's:

Example 264

The *auftakt* is brought about in a most charming way in the first *Allegro* theme, through the quaver rest on its first beat:

Example 265

In the second *Allegro* theme it is impossible to shape the *auftakt* directly. Still it sounds as a melodic sixth, formed through a bridging group preceding the theme from E to G sharp:

173

Example 266

This *auftakt* sixth is also heard in the third *Rondo theme*:

Example 267

and is especially emphasized in the *Adagio* theme:

Example 268

In fact, the beginning of the *Adagio* is a kind of improvisation on the idea of the *auftakt*:

Example 269

And, by the way, the melodic contour of this shape:

Example 270

is a reiteration of a little phrase which first emerged in the figuration of the *Allegro* (Example 271)—where, as a proof of its motivic message, it is sounded five times in succession.

Example 271

In its compass from A to E, with the D sharp in between, this little phrase spells a kind of chromatic version of the basic model.

16

Motivic Dissolution in the D Minor Sonata, Op. 31 No. 2

A N unusual structural feature—we might almost call it architectural resolution through motivic dissolution—becomes visible in the Sonata in D minor, Op. 31 No. 2. The opening period reads:

Example 272

In order to establish the pattern from a thematic point of view, we have divided the opening measures into three segments. Segment I, in an improvising *Adagio* tempo, is formed by an *arpeggio*. Segment II, the most substantial of the three, is formed through a *series of identical particles*. Segment III is a *melismatic phrase* consisting of a *turn plus a particle*. The summation of these three shapes forms the thematic pattern of the whole sonata. Segment II, however, seems to be decisive. Here one little group forms the essence, and we will call it the *prime shape*. This prime shape appears first in D, is repeated, and then transposed to G.

Let us look more deeply into the structure of the prime shape. Though the four particles of which it consists seem identical, they nevertheless create quite different effects. For, in relation to the bass, the first of these particles forms a consonance, while the following particles form dissonances:

Example 273

In the first particle, therefore, the opening note, the A, remains without a doubt, the melodic pivot. The line formed by the following particles, however, may be heard melodically either as a series of consonant resolutions (by connecting their second notes), henceforth referred to as element (**a**):

Example 274

or as a series of dissonances (by connecting their first notes), to be called element (**b**):

By letting these two shapes sound side by side, the theme of the *Finale* emerges:

Thus, in this sonata, the architectural resolution into the tonic-dominant phenomenon is achieved through a dissolution of its prime motif into two elements.

Element *a* appears in the *Allegro* as:

Example 275

(a)

while in the *Finale* it appears as:

(b)

This same shape emerges in the second movement, the *Adagio*, as a kind of mirror form:

From these three motivic variants the three movements of the sonata are developed.

The opening theme, after having been brought to a half close, is resumed and varied in an expanded arc and on a new harmonic basis. This second half of the opening section reads:

Example 276

It is interesting to note that in this whole opening section the harmonic course appears far removed from any traditional scheme. The opening period starts with the dominant rather than with the tonic, and moreover with the 6/3 of the dominant. It also ends with the dominant in a half close. This in itself would not seem unusual, as openings in the dominant are, after all, frequently heard in the music of Beethoven and other composers of that time. However, after a period framed by the dominant, one might expect a quick, definite establishment of the tonic. But instead, the composer finds himself in C major, or to be more specific, on the minor seventh of the basic key. He thereupon fights his way gradually through the usual progressions of secondary dominants to the 6/4 of D minor. And only now is the cadencing conclusion into the tonic achieved. Before this, during the whole opening section, the tonic was heard merely as a (so to speak) passing utterance. In contrast, the following section, with its rhythmical strictness, is at last firmly centred in D minor:

Example 277

Example 278

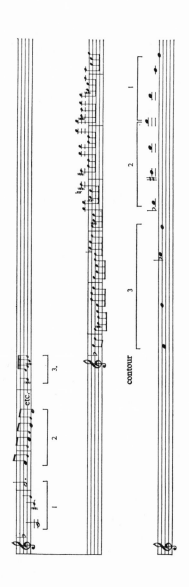

Hence this section would appear to be the first 'real' thematic section. For the opening section which precedes it, both in its unusual harmonic course and its constant change of tempo (from *Largo* to *Allegro* to *Adagio* to *Largo* to *Allegro*), bears, as do so many opening sections in Beethoven's music, the character of an improvisational introduction. And in common with all these 'introductions' this one spells in outline all the structural ideas from which the work is built.

First, as described above, it already contains in its first period all the prime features from which the thematic pattern of the sonata is developed. In its second period these features are taken over as a part of a design so startling in symmetric logic that we do not hesitate to outline it in full.

The prime features are spelled in this second period through the contour. This contour mirrors in contrary motion the whole shaping of the first period. It truly 'mirrors' these motivic features; that is, it shows them in reversed succession of their first appearance; first segment III, the *turn*; then segment II, the *prime shape*; and finally segment I, the *arpeggio*. One has only to read Example 278 back and forth from the centre, to see the whole scheme as an image and its reflection.

Moreover, the introductory section also produces the larger design from which the whole architecture of the work is built. Let us again start from the pattern. It consists of the three familiar segments: I, an arpeggio; II, the prime shape formed through a stepwise progression from A to D; and III, that melismatic phrase consisting of the turn plus particle.

Now, this very pattern represents in various combinations the essence of all the thematic schemes of the sonata. First, following the 'introduction', there is the main section of the *Allegro*. Its thematic shaping is brought about, as is readily seen in the example below, by a summation of segment I plus segment III:

Example 279

Segment II, however, seems to be missing, or at least it does not suggest itself immediately. But it too is soon discovered as the contour of the bass line. There it sounds (in contrary motion) in ponderous steps:

Example 280

That Beethoven really regarded this contour of the bass (representing the prime shape) as an essential feature, is certified by the fact that this same shape is immediately reiterated in emphatic contrapuntal imitation in the upper voices also, as can be seen from the following outline:

Example 281

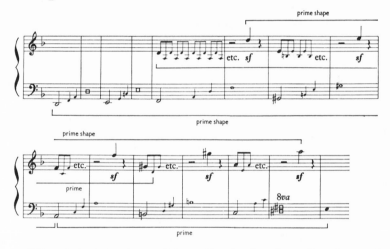

This whole design is certainly an illuminating piece of contrapuntal art. Okeghem or Josquin des Prés, the great masters of the polyphonic era, might well have taken pride in such a shaping. And here the effectiveness of the contrapuntal treatment is heightened by concentrated motivic combination.

The following section is built from a series of particles in different variants. However, the main elements of arpeggio, prime shape and turn are included as well:

Example 282

The turn then appears in the next group, for once as the main melodic line, followed by the contrary motion of the prime shape:

Example 283

This shape is then transferred to the bass. In general it is interesting to note that in this entire section the melodic course is formed as an uninterrupted series of particles, even if sometimes this inner substance has first to be unravelled, in order to become visible:

Example 284

The last of these shapes into which the *Allegro* finally flows, is the most significant (and by the way, it is another example of double counterpoint). In the following example we quote this shape from its reiteration in the recapitulation, as the pitch at which it there emerges is in itself revealing:

Example 285

For these figures represent the two 'dissolved' elements of the prime shape:

Example 286

the inversions of which form the *Finale* theme.

Returning to our thematic pattern, we may turn to the second movement, the *Adagio*. The melodic line of its opening period reads:

Example 287

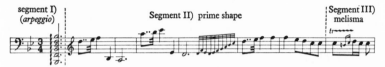

and so we see that the *Allegro* pattern is presented clearly as the model for this theme too. For segment I, the arpeggio, forms its beginning, and segment III, the melismatic phrase, forms the end. Therefore, between these two, segment II has to be embedded. And indeed, the two corresponding shapes of this segment follow each other in the *Adagio* theme, just as they did in the *Allegro*. Segment II of the *Allegro*:

Example 288

which, as described previously, appears in the *Adagio* transformed into:

(b)

is in the *Allegro* followed by:

Example 289

which therefore has to appear in the *Adagio* in analogous transformation as:

In the *Allegro*, segment II appears twice, and this procedure is repeated in the *Adagio*; here, however, the second appearance is postponed until after segment III has been sounded.

These two shapes from the *Allegro*, appearing there in D and G, also form the pattern of the *Finale* theme. However, since in the *Finale* segment II is 'dissolved' into the two elements, the analogy here assumes the following picture:

Example 290

And here too, the other features, arpeggio and turn, are not missing. They appear in the bass: the arpeggio through the figurations, the turn as its contour:

Example 291

But the design of the *Allegro* introduction is repeated in the *Finale* in an even wider sense, to form the backbone of its whole architecture. First, note the following feature. In the *Allegro*, the opening period is followed by a second arpeggio in C, which connects it to the next group:

Example 292

This same idea is resumed in the *Finale*. When here the first *Finale* theme is brought to a close by the interpolation of a kind of codetta, the same arpeggio in C, now transformed into the tempo and rhythm of the *Finale*, introduces the following section:

184

Example 293

But apart from this detail, let us investigate the substance of the codetta. It forms a repetition of the last bars of the *Finale* theme with two accentuated chromatic passages included. And it is of interest to discover that these passages, in their descent from A to D and from D to G (sharp), form a clear replica of the two *Allegro* prime shapes, now appearing as 'chromatic versions':

Example 294

Only with the following, however, do we approach the most revealing part of the analogy. For in the first movement the rise of the two figures derived from the prime shape appears extended in the next period through a leap to the high F:

Example 295

And even this feature is transferred literally to the *Finale*. At the very point when the sonata draws to a conclusion, the codetta is repeated (bars 373–385)—but repeated with the leap to the high F included. Thus the work is led to its climax.

The leap from A through D to F forms a sixth. And this 'melodic sixth', so often used in a similar sense in Beethoven's works, is applied here too, from the beginning of the sonata, as a specific motivic feature. In fact, the work opens with the sixth heard through the arpeggio:

Example 296

Later it emerges emphatically as the structural characteristic of the *Finale* theme, both in its detail and in its contour:

Example 297

This same sixth rises in numerous other significant shapings within the sonata, and always emphasizes one pitch, mirroring the beginning of the *Finale*:

Example 298

And this melodic sixth is seen finally in the relationship between the sonata's movements, of which the keys* are:

Example 299

* *cf. The Thematic Process in Music*, Chapter 8, 'Thematic Key Relations'.

17
Methods of Transformation*

IN this chapter some particular observations and examples are added which may help to visualize the methods of transformation more clearly. A little incident in connection with the analysis of the *Waldstein* Sonata given in an earlier chapter may furnish an introduction. When this brief analysis was read to a circle of musicians, the question was raised whether a certain shape representing a new theme, or at least a new thematic thought, had not been forgotten or omitted in the analysis, and whether by including this shape, the concept of thematic uniformity on which the analysis of the *Waldstein* was centred, would not be destroyed.

The shape referred to is the group at the conclusion of the sonata's exposition:

Example 300

First of all, the validity of our analysis is certainly not endangered by the omission of this shape. For the shape is neither a new theme nor a new thematic thought. Viewed from a truly structural angle, it represents merely a continuation of these cadencing figurations which fill the extended section of the second theme:

Example 301

* This chapter should be regarded as an annexe of 'Various Categories of Transformation' in *The Thematic Process in Music*.

This becomes clear once we restore the phrasing of the alleged new thought to the original triplets. Then the group, instead of reading:

Example 302

(a)

simply reads:

(b)

Thus the 'new shape' reduces itself at best to another variant of an old one, to a continuation of the preceding figurations. Nevertheless, it is true that although the motivic substance in the new thought would seem to be identical to that of the old, its melodic appearance has changed essentially. And it is precisely the melodic appearance of a shape which endows it with musical meaning.

When Beethoven saw his glittering figurations extended over this whole section, he must have felt somewhat disturbed by such a charming yet over-long uniformity. On the other hand, what he did not wish to do, at this advanced stage of the exposition, was to overburden his design with a truly new thematic section. Instead, he annexed this coda, using a little device at once simple and effective. He lengthened the first note of the triplets by a fraction,

Example 303

from  to

and through this minute, almost unnoticeable alteration changed to an incredible degree the whole picture and melodic appeal of this part of the score.

However, effects like these constitute the very difficulty which confronts us in the elementary stage of thematic analysis, for it is only natural that one hesitates to recognize the inner structural identity of shapes of which the outer appearance is so different. Still, it is precisely this difference in which the essence of all structural forming lies. And once the first enthusiasm of having discovered the law of thematic unity has passed, one should not be disappointed if that unity is not carried out literally throughout a composition, if some divergent elements also become visible in shapes which the analysing mind almost wishes were identical. Besides, if here and there a few notes emerge, as often happens, through which the pattern of analogy seems interrupted, it may mean merely that another thematic feature has been combined or interwoven with the first. In fact one might say that the less recognizable the inner identity of shapes appears through a contrasting surface, the more effective this shaping may be considered from an artistic angle. At any rate, the great achievement of the composers of the classical period was that they were able to preserve the motivic substance but at the same time transform it to a new melodic appearance.

1. MOTIVIC DYNAMICS

That dynamics often play an essential part in underlining thematic shapes has been shown repeatedly in this analysis; and Beethoven, it seems, had a particular liking for this technique. In some cases, however, he applies dynamic marks as the very means of making motifs audible which otherwise might not have been noticed at all.

The *Kreutzer* Sonata furnishes an interesting illustration of this type. When the opening of the first movement's *Presto* is reiterated at the entrance of the coda, the middle segment of the theme is extended to a larger group, reading:

Example 304

Eleven *sforzati* shine out from this line, and from an outward view there seems to be no reason why these eleven notes only should be accentuated and why other notes (indicated by a cross) should be passed over. One could of course say that the composer simply wished to infuse the performer with an emphatic impulse, but at the same time was not meticulous about whether a few notes more or less received a *sforzato.* Such casualness, however, is certainly not in keeping with Beethoven's almost fanatical precision in dynamic notation. The true explanation is rather that the *sforzati* are supposed to make two motivic shapes stand out in bold relief. In the opening theme this group reads:

Example 305

Apart from the underlying pedal on E and A, the kernel of this line is a diminished fifth formed by a stepwise ascent ('step-ladder'):

Example 306

Now through the *sforzati* this ascent of a diminished fifth is heard twice in the resumption (notated as an augmented fourth):

Example 307

while without such motivic dynamics these motivic fifths would have remained unnoticed in the continuous line of phrasing.

2. TRANSFORMATION IN THE D MAJOR SONATA, OP. 10, NO. 3

Just as contrapuntal skill and knowledge of harmony are familiar to any schooled musician, so the ability to recognize the typical thematic transformations from a given shape could and should be applied to the classics. Such a technique could then be useful as a clue to the deciphering of the structure of any classical work. At least the thematic elements should be recognized at first glance. For instance, by extracting the two prime cells from the opening theme of Beethoven's D major sonata:

Example 308

one would then immediately recognize the opening of the *Finale*:

Example 309

as a counterpoint of (a) and (b) in inversion. Similarly, one would recognize the opening of the *Adagio*:

Example 310

as the transposition of the same shapes into the minor. Or the opening of the minuet:

Example 311

would be recognized as a variant of the same feature with an ascending sixth (inversion of the basic third) as an *auftakt*; and this *auftakt* is already announced in the second *Allegro* theme, which otherwise spells the same idea:

Example 312

One would finally recognize one of the later groups as a summation of the same *auftakt*:

Example 313

plus the opening bar:

in augmentation:

Example 314

This, by the way, represents one of the rare cases in Beethoven's music where an augmentation is not heard in contour, but in its pure form.

3. DIFFERENT VOICES MINGLE IN THE E MAJOR SONATA, OP. 14 NO. 1

One of the techniques through which motifs sometimes assume new appearances requires a short description of its own. It is the technique whereby a motivic shape emerges by the connection of certain points of different voices into one line.* An example from the E major sonata, Op. 14 No. 1 may demonstrate this convincingly. First, however, a brief analytical outline of the opening of the work is necessary. The first thematic group† reads:

Example 315

* Cf. *The Thematic Process in Music*, p.90, regarding Op. 27 No. 2.
† This theme reminds one of the last theme in the *Finale* of the *Pathétique*:

and there is a very natural explanation for this. The *Pathétique* is Op. 13, while the E major sonata is Op. 14, No. 1. Beethoven was obviously so interested in

This pattern is formed by three rising fourths (the last a 'filled' one in a characteristic rhythm), with a sixth between them. The filled fourth —B, C sharp, D sharp, E—forms also the contour of the lower voices. These fourths are continued in the next group:

Example 316

a fact which becomes quickly visible by contracting its figurations to chords:

Example 317

Then the following group reiterates these figurations in a slower tempo:

Example 318

Compare:

Example 319

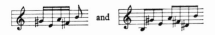

This last bar however, shows the two particles simultaneously:

---

this shape, which was brought about as the last result of the design of the *Pathétique*, but from which at this late stage of the work he could not draw any structural conclusions, that he decided to write a new sonata commencing with this shape. And it is especially significant, from the point of view of our method of analysis, to see what different architectural meanings evolve from these almost identical shapes. In the *Pathétique*, these fourths and fifths were the goal to which the original thirds were finally transformed, while in the E major sonata they are the prime cells from which a quite different picture is developed.

xample 320

ıd so reminds one of the opening group:

xample 321

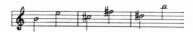

[ere, in trying to combine both features, Beethoven seems to have been ırced to omit the middle part of the opening. The succeeding group resents a first indication of the mingling of voices mentioned above:

xample 322

y connecting the alto line with two notes of the soprano, the opening :oup emerges again, though in interversion.
ompare the opening group:

xample 323

ith the line formed by connecting alto and soprano:

xample 324

ı the following period the opening theme is repeated, partly in ıversion:

xample 325

After this, the secondary theme is introduced, the rising sixth from the opening theme (now filled in chromatically) being its structural centre:

Example 326

Now we are approaching the heart of the matter. The theme of the second movement reads as follows:

Example 327

This shape, of course, must be understood as a new one—that is, specifically as the theme of the *Allegretto*. But then let us search for the features by means of which this theme is connected to the first movement. By linking the alto of bar 1 to the soprano of bar 2, then the alto of bar 3 to the soprano of bar 4, a line emerges, reading:

Example 328

which makes this *Allegretto* theme appear as a clear replica of the opening theme of the sonata, interwoven with the secondary theme. This amazing feature was brought about by drawing a line between elements of two independent voices.

4. THEMATIC CONSISTENCY AND TRANSFORMATION IN THE G MAJOR SONATA, OP. 14 NO. 2

In *The Thematic Process in Music* it is demonstrated how the theme of the second movement of this sonata turns out to be an inversion of the first movement's beginning, greatly reduced in tempo and phrasing.

Let us turn here to the *Finale*, which Beethoven, against all tradition, termed a scherzo. Recalling the opening of the sonata:

Example 329

one may at first glance be at a loss to detect any similarity or relationship between this and the *Finale* theme, which reads:

Example 330

With the extraordinary speed of this movement one might easily recognize the accentuated D to D of these bars (see the asterisks in the example) as a recollection of the octave with which the first movement opens. The next notes of the opening shape were:

Example 331

and as can be seen in Example 330, these now appear in the left hand immediately after the octave.

Then the whole group is repeated, with one significant variation: the corresponding notes no longer read as above, but as:

Example 332

Thus as indicated by the brackets in the two examples, the A sharp to B is replaced by the corresponding F sharp to G. From this point of view—which, it must be understood, is not formulated at random, but is after all based on a strict principle of symmetry—the contour of this whole *Finale* group would read:

Example 333

an obvious replica of the sonata's opening. Yet we must be objective. For were such an example to stand isolated within the massive stock of Beethoven's structures, it would be idle play to point to such an alleged relationship. But since, in the light of our foregoing investigation, we know that it was Beethoven's regular procedure to develop one movement from the other, we cannot help recognizing the same phenomenon in this case also.

In returning to our example, we may wish to discover whether the continuation of the work confirms our supposition. The group following the one just discussed commences in the first movement as:

Example 334

and reads in the third movement:

Example 335

thus proving a similarity of kernel beyond a doubt. We may remember that this almost literal analogy was also seen between this same group and the corresponding one of the second movement.*

The next groups of the *Finale* elaborate no less on the same basic motif:

Example 336

Example 337

The original idea can readily be seen from the contour.

[* See *The Thematic Process in Music*, pp. 75–77.—ED.]

After a repetition of this whole section, the groups of the second section follow:

Example 338

The analogy in substance of this second subject of the *Finale* to the second subject of the first movement is clear:

Example 339

but the above quotation from Op. 14 No. 2 is an example of a method of transformation which cannot be classified under any scheme.

We have to realize, however, that all transformations which constitute thematic structure show at least some traces of such a non-thematic quality. This aloofness from any rigid schematism is the fact which separates the principle of motivic permeation, as the structural technique of the classical period, from the principle of contrapuntal imitation in the polyphonic era. The polyphonists inverted, reverted, augmented their thematic shapes literally—in short they imitated the chosen thought in various ways through the different voices. The classical composers also based their compositional process on a given substance, but they changed it in the course of the work to ever new characters, new themes, to a new appearance.

5. ARCHITECTURAL RESOLUTION THROUGH THEMATIC TRANSFORMATION

Before concluding our present description of methods of transformation, a last important feature should not be forgotten—the often-described phenomenon of architectural resolution. For as has been described, composers not only use the thematic technique to develop the necessary variety in a composition, they also build their compositions according to an overall pattern. Beethoven, in accordance with this idea, usually changes the basic cell-motif in the last movement of a work. He changes it into a shape only slightly different in outward appearance, but essentially different in its inner substance and therefore in its architectural consequence. He changes it in order to make of it an emphatic expression of the tonic-dominant phenomenon.

If, as demonstrated earlier, throughout the whole of the first movement of the *Pathétique* a thematic picture is developed based on the following cells:

Example 340

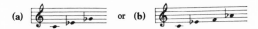

and if in the *Finale* this is altered to:

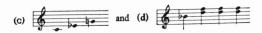

then through this inconspicuous change an entirely new spirit arises in the listener's mind.

Perhaps the whole story of the *Appassionata* can be envisaged in these minute changes:

Example 341

This is not only interesting from an architectural and spiritual point of view, but also from a specific technical angle. The reason why these resolutions carry such weight is that they represent cases in which not only the phrasing and character of a motif are changed, but, so to say, the material of the motif, namely its intervals. Such a change of interval, through which not only the appearance of a motif is changed, but its very substance, proves to be far more decisive in its implications than any other type of transformation. And this type of transformation we call thematic resolution.

Beethoven's 'thematic resolutions' have almost invariably one characteristic in common: structurally they transform a shape which has a quality of discord into an expression of perfect harmony—for instance, a line centred around a chord of the seventh is resolved into a triad, or a complex chordal progression into one rooted in the tonic-dominant relation. Correspondingly, in the dramatic–emotional sense Beethoven's resolutions lead from tension to release, from compulsion to liberation, from the tragic to the joyous. For these transformations on which Beethoven's architectural plans are centred, 'resolution' is therefore a fitting expression.

18

Beethoven's Sketches

SKETCHES OF THE D MINOR SONATA, OP. 31 NO. 2

An analysis of the Sonata in D minor, Op. 31 No. 2, was given in the last chapter but one. It may be of interest, as a conclusion, to compare the text of the sonata with the sketches made for it by Beethoven. The first part of the *Allegro* in the sketch-book reads:

Example 342

to which, for comparison, the same part as it appears in the finished work may be added:

Example 343

The first difference we see is that in the conclusion of the opening period the melismatic ornament:

Example 344

is not present in the sketch. Therefore, quite naturally, from a thematic point of view, the corresponding shape in the following thematic section of the finished work:

Example 345

does not appear in the sketch either. This may be regarded as self-evident; but now comes an interesting point. As we may remember from our earlier analysis, a third feature is also included in the finished work. This feature is the prime shape of the work; it emerged in the middle part of the opening theme (both in the sketch and in the finished work) as:

Example 346

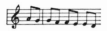

In the finished work, this shape appears also in the following section, here in contrary motion, interwoven as the contour of the bass, the original G natural being altered to G sharp:

Example 347

Moreover, a few bars later this same contrary motion of the prime shape also rises as an imitating counterpoint in the soprano line, and now emphasized by *sforzati*:

Example 348

Now this whole feature—that is, the reappearance of the prime shape in this section—is non-existent in the sketch—not even the remotest intimation of it is traceable there.

What does this tell us? The motif in question, which cannot be traced in the sketched version, even in indication, must, therefore, have been *worked into* the finished composition. For shapes like this one, appearing as a large arc in the contour of a long period, and with such contrapuntal complexity, cannot emerge just at random. They have to be planned, to be built. The sketch shows the outline as it grew from the composer's first inspired improvisation. True, this improvisation is completely thematic in itself. Almost too thematic, one might say, as it follows the one motivic tune—that is, the opening arpeggio—almost to the point of exhaustion. (This is somewhat reminiscent of the motivic tune laid bare in the *Pathétique*.) However, when the sonata had to be shaped into its final form, Beethoven did not feel satisfied that, in such a large section of a work, just this element was missing which in other parts of the composition is developed into its main feature, the prime shape. He therefore worked it into his first improvised version as a contour. In this way he was able to strengthen, consciously, that original version.